虎倒流

Koto Ryu

骨法術

Koppo Jutsu

相傳之巻

Soden No Maki

Striking Techniques
of the
Tiger Felling School
Transmission Scroll

Transcription Kazuhiro Iida
Translation Eric Shahan

- This document has been translated for historical research purposes only.
- It should not be used as a training methodology.
- The document contains a number of historical errors.
- The document is extremely vague on some points and notes have been added to highlight possible interpretations.
- The original document will be reproduced, followed by a Japanese transcription and an English translation.

Striking Techniques
of the
Koto Ryu Tiger Felling School
Transmission Scroll

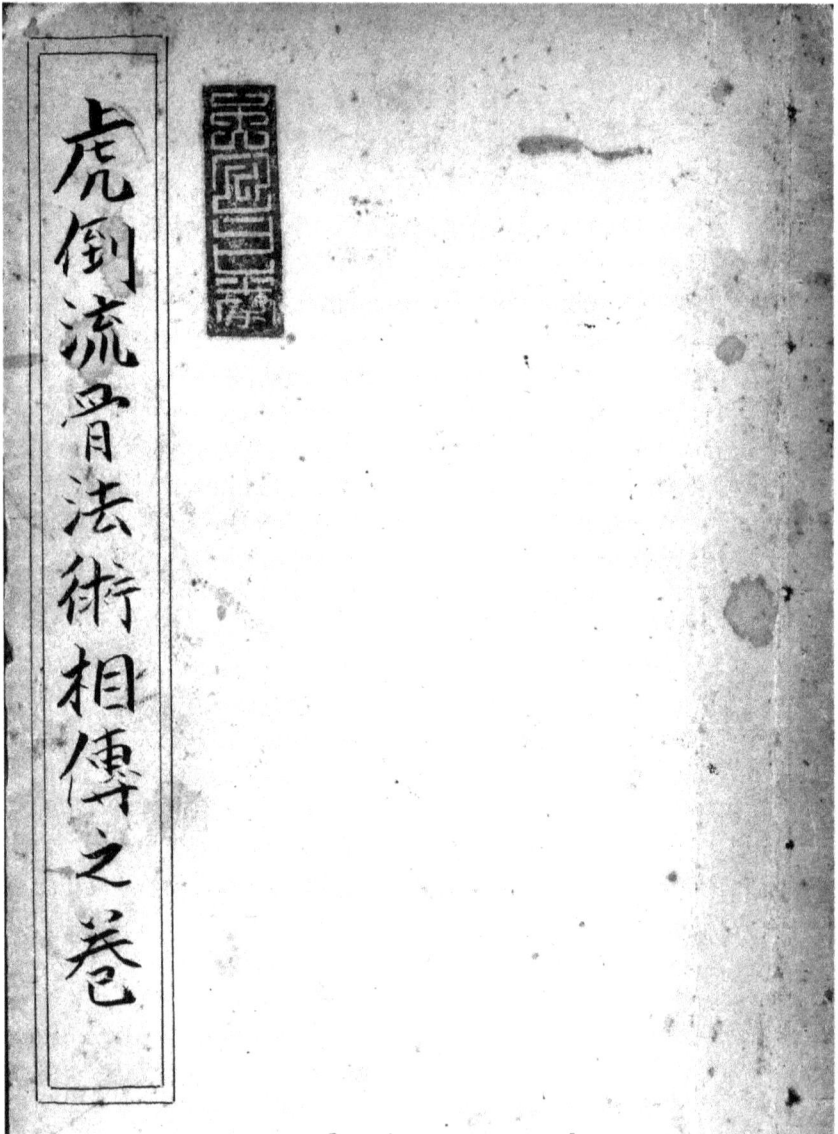

虎倒流骨法術相傳之巻

虎倒流骨法術相傳之巻

姚玉虎ハ骨指術、飛鳥術、鈷盤君術ノ祖師ハ中国ニテハ古クヨリ伝ヘラレタ

如ク玉虎ガ此術ニ最モ勝レ骨指術ニテ多クヲ倒シ、又虎ヲ鈷盤術

ニテ重膓ヲ買ハレ骨指術ニテ倒セシ程ノ達人ナル事ハ中国ニテハヨク知

ラレ居ル也此術代々伝ヘラレ張武連ニ至リ漢国ニ帰化セシ如ク、武連ハ

此術ヲ武勝ニ伝フ武勝ハ武連ノ子也。姚玉虎ハ今ダ年少ノ美女タリ中国

語史歴ノ如ク姚玉虎ヨリ伝ヘラレタル為メ玉虎骨指術ヲ祖トス、武

連ノ子武勝ハ我朝天和天皇ニ癸亥年九月漢ノ孫仁師百済ト戰

フ此時武勝ハ百済ノ武將タリ時ニ百済戰ニ敗レテ百済王餘豐高

麗ニ走ル張武勝ハ從者ト共ニ新国ニ逃レ来ル武勝ハ骨指術、飛鳥術

鈷盤君投術、薙刀術、十八型中国唐打術ノ達人タリ之ヲ新国ニ広メタ

ルヲ新国骨法術ノ祖トスノ記録残レリ然レ共天文年間以前ノ記録ハ

明ラカデナイガ武勝ノ子孫ガ坂上田村麿デアルト云フ記録モアリ政ニ田

虎倒流骨法術相傳之巻
せんばん

姚玉虎、骨指術、飛鳥術、鉆磐術の祖師は中国にては古くより伝えられた如く、玉虎が此の術にい最も勝れ骨指術にて多くを倒し、又虎を鉆磐術にて重傷を負わし骨指術にて倒せし程の達人なる事は中国にてはよく知られ居る也。此の術、代々伝えられ、張武連に至り、漢国に帰化せし如く、武連は此の術を武勝に伝う。武勝は武連の子也。姚玉虎は今だ年少の美女たり。中国語史歴の如く姚玉虎より伝えられたる為、玉虎骨指術を祖とす。武連の子、武勝は我が朝、天和天皇に葵亥年九月漢の孫仁師百済と戦う。此の時、武勝は百済の武将たり時に百済戦い敗れて百済王餘豊、高麗に走る。張武勝は従者と共に我国に逃れ来る。武勝は骨指術、飛鳥術、鉆磐投術、薙刀術、十八型中国唐打術の達人たり。然れ共、天文年間以前の記録は明らかでないが、武勝の子孫が坂上田村麿であると云う記録もあり。故に

Striking Techniques
of the
Koto Ryu Tiger Felling School
Transmission Scroll

Long ago in China a woman named Cho Gyokko, the jeweled tiger developed a school of fighting that included:

Kosshi Jutsu – A type of Jujutsu that relies on the strength in the fingers
Hicho Jutsu – Jumping attacks and retreats
Senban Jutsu – A type of shuriken technique

These techniques have been passed down through the generations from days of old. Gyokko used these techniques, which were the most powerful and effective Kosshi Jutsu in order to topple many opponents. The story of how she used Senban Jutsu to first injure a tiger before killing it with Kosshi Jutsu is well known in China.

The teachings of this school were passed down from one generation to the next until they were transmitted to a man named Cho Buren. When he eventually returned to the Han Kingdom, Buren passed his teachings onto a man named Busho. Busho was the son of Buren. At this time Cho, the Jeweled Tiger was a beautiful young girl. According to Chinese history, in order for her to pass these techniques on she was made the founder of Gyokko Ryu Kosshi Jutsu.

In September of 663, during the reign of Emperor Tenji, Busho, the son of Buren fought the Chinese forces led by the general Sonjinshi at Kudara. Sonjinshi was leading the [combined forces of Gogureyo and Silla] against Baekje.[1]

---

[1] Since The Battle of Baekgang 白村江の戦い occurred from August 27-28 in 663, the Emperor would have been the Tenji Tenno 天智天皇 who lived 626 – 671. The original Japanese text lists the Emperor as the Tenwa Tenno 天和天皇 who lived 1681 – 1684.

During this battle Busho served as a general from the kingdom of Baekje [known as Kudara in Japanese]. He was defeated in the battle of Kudara and Prince Buyeo Pund fled to Gorureyo. Cho Busho fled with his troops to our country, Japan.

Busho was an expert at:

Kosshi Jutsu	–	A type of Jujutsu that relies on the strength in the fingers
Hicho Jutsu	–	Jumping attacks and retreats
Senban Jutsu	–	A type of shuriken technique
Naginata Jutsu	–	Techniques using a halberd

The 18 striking arts of Tang China

He was responsible for spreading these teachings in Japan. That is why he is recorded as being the father of Koppo Jutsu (A kind of Jujutsu that that relies on joint manipulation) in our country.

The records preceding the Tenbun Era of 1532-1535 are unclear, however we do have a record that Sakanoue No Tamuramaru was the grandson/descendant of Busho. For that reason Tamuramaru was considered to be Chinese.

村麿ハ中国帰化人デアルト云フ事ニナル斯ク如ク骨指術ハ古来カラ伝

ヘラレタガ飛鳥術ハ後飛切ノ術ト称サレ銘敏石術ハ銭ヲ投ゲトナリ

手裏剣術ト名称ヲ類目ヘテ伝ヘラレタ之ノ術ガ一般ニ伝ヘラレナカッ

タ原因ハ主トシテ忍術者ノ秘伝トセラレタ故デアル其記録トシテ保

元元年両子七月源為義斬首セラルヽヤ其臣源武部亜朝

行伊賀ノ岩ヶ尾山ニ亡命シ入道シテ法玄仙人ト称シ仙人ヨリ一指ヲ以テ

人ヲ倒ス又其次ヲ見タル者ナシト云フ則チ飛鳥骨法術ヲ行ヒ骨法術ヲ

行ヒ以テ人ヲ倒セシ如シ王虎飛鳥骨法術ト称スル事ヲ考ヘテモ

姚王虎ノ骨法術タル事明カナリ法玄仙人ニ何テ学ビシ童法入道

コニ伊加冥流忍術ノ初祖トモ云フベシ

坂上大
郎国重

坂上田村麿後裔玉虎指頭術飛龍銀達人
天文十年名見鈴山城魯土天乃十年田毒降ト戦ヒ敗ヒ罰死ス

国重ハ玉虎指頭術飛鳥新銀達人

佐々木源太夫員安
天文年間紀州玉心流骨法術祖

佐々木五郎右エ門輝頼
義鑑流骨指術祖
瓜生別宮義鑑房

河内守義鑑
頭津河内瓜生坂生

童王観律師

播州本体玉虎流虎倒流剣法術祖
戸田一心斉

出雲本体玉虎流骨法術祖
鈴木大善大夫迄政

深尾角馬重義

田村麿は中国帰化人であると云う事になる。斯くの如く骨指術は古来から伝えられたが飛鳥術は後、飛切の術と称され、銚磐術は銭投げとなり、手裏剣術と名称を替えて伝えられた。之の術が一般に伝えられなかった原因は主として忍術者の秘伝とせられた故である。其記録として保元元年丙子七月、源為義斬首せらる、や其臣、源式部亟朝行、伊賀岩尾山に亡命、入道して法玄仙人と称し、仙人よく一指を以て人を倒す。又、其姿を見たる者なしと云う。 則ち飛鳥術を行い、骨法術を行い、以て人を倒せし如し玉虎飛鳥骨法術と称する事を考えても姚玉虎の骨法術たる事、明かなり。 法玄仙人に付て学びし竜法入道こ、に伊賀流忍術の初祖とも云うべし。

The techniques of Kosshi Jutsu were passed down as they were originally taught, but Hicho Jutsu became Hisetsu no Jutsu. Senban Jutsu became first Sen-nage Jutsu and then later Shuriken Jutsu.

Kosshi Jutsu → Kosshi Jutsu
Hicho Jutsu → Hisetsu Jutsu
Senban Jutsu → Sen-nage Jutsu → Shuriken Jutsu

The main reason these techniques were not more widely taught is due to the secrecy amongst Ninjutsu Sha. The only record we have regarding this is from July of the first year of Hogen 1156 when Minamoto no Tameyoshi 1096 – 1156 was beheaded. His retainer, Minamoto Shikibu no Jo, escaped to Mt. Iwao in Iga Domain. There he took the tonsure and the name Hogen Sennin.

You often hear of Sennin toppling people with one finger. Further, it is said that you can never find a person that met a Sennin. Since the Sennin are famous for being able to employ Hicho Jutsu and Kosshi Jutsu in an instant, these techniques are often referred to as Gyokko Hicho Koppo Jutsu, or The Flying Bird Jujutsu of the Jeweled Tiger School. However they are clearly the Koppo art of Cho Gyokko, the Jeweled Tiger.

Ryuho "Eight Dragons" who studied under Hogen Sennin could probably be considered to be the first master of Iga School Ninjutsu.

Japanese Lineage Chart

坂上太郎国重 ——————————— 僧玉観律師 ——
  坂上田村麿後裔、玉虎指頭術飛龍剣の達人　　国重重臣玉虎指頭
  天文十年岩見館山城勇士天門十辛丑年五月、　術飛鳥斬剣達人
  大内義隆と戦い敗れて戦死す。

佐々木源太夫貞安—佐々木五郎右衛門輝頼—代々紀州方面に残る
  攝津河内瓜生城主　　義鑑流骨指術租

河内守義鑑┬瓜生判官義鑑房 - - - 代々子孫に伝え、現在尚残る。

   ├戸田一心斉 - - - - - - - -当流也。
   　播州本体玉虎流、虎倒流骨法術、銛磐投術租

   └鈴木大善太夫近政 - -　深尾角馬重義 - -代々伝う
   　出雲本体玉虎流、　　寛文年間打拳骨法、
   　出雲流骨法術租　　　井蛙流剣法租

Lineage Chart in English

| Sakanoue Taro Kunishige | – Descended from Sakanoue Tamuramaru. He was a master of Gyokko Shito Jutsu Hiryuken, or Jeweled Tiger Toppling the Head With One Finger Flying Dragon Sword. [He was born?] in the 10th year of Tenbun, 1452, at Iwami Castle [Tateyama ?] he died fighting Ouchi Yoshitaka 1507 – 1551 in May of 1541.

↓

| Sogyokkan Ritsushi | – A top retainer of Shigekuni. A master of Gyokko Ryu Shito Jutsu and Hicho Zanken, or Flying Bird Cutting Sword.

↓

| Sasaki Gentafu Sadayasu | – Head of Uryo Castle in the Kawauchi of Settsu Domain.

↓

| Sasaki Goro Uemon | – Founder of Gikan Ryu Kosshi Jutsu
This tradition is still being passed on in the Kishu Region.

↓

| Guardian of Kawauchi Gikan | → | Uryo Hankan Gikanbo |

↓

Continues to be passed on in the
Kishu Area, exists even today

| Toda Isshinsai |
Founder of Banshu Hontai Gyokko Ryu, Kotoryu Koppo Jutsu,
Senban Nage Jutsu. This tradition continues in the Toda Family.

| Suzuki Taizen Tafukinsei | → | Mio Kakuma Shigenori |

Founder of Izumo Hontai Gyokko Ryu and Izumo Ryu Koppo Jutsu

During the Kanbun Era 1661 - 1673 he developed a style of Dakken Koppo, or Striking Bone Techniques, and founded Seia School of Sword fighting. This tradition continues to be passed on.

10

Translator's Notes:

骨法術 **Koppo Jutsu** – This document states that Busho is considered to be the father of Koppo Jutsu. It is not clear why the name changed from Kosshi to Koppo. Possibly to indicate a lesser reliance on the fingers alone.

武芸十八般 **Bugei Juhappan** – The 18 Martial Arts/ The 18 Weapons of War. The documents states that Busho was adept at the 18 striking arts, but it is not clear if this is referring to the famous 18 Martial Arts or to 18 types of boxing. It is probably the former, meaning that he had experience in using 14 other weapons. This can include all the major weapons like spear, sword, and bow as well as techniques like swimming or Ninjutsu.

仙人 **Sennin**- A mountain ascetic. The first Kanji of Sennin is made up of the elements of *person* 人 beside *mountain* 山.

Sakanoue Taro Kunishige – The information under his name is very difficult to dissect. There was no Tateyama Castle until 1580 and Iwami Castle is written 岩見 instead of 石見. The brave warriors of Tenmon died in May of 1541, though the battle seems to have begun in 1542 and lasted until 1543. It is not clear who "the brave warriors of Tenmon" were.
The battle where Sakanoue died may have been The Siege of Toda Castle 月山富田城の戦い *Gassan Toda-jō no Tatakai*. This battle was long and occurred in stages lasting a total of 16 months from 1565 ~ 1567.

虎倒流骨法術位取

右正眼

左正眼

虎倒流骨法術位取
Koto Ryu Koppo Jutsu Kurai Tori

Koto School Striking Techniques : Stances

左正眼 Hidari Seigan	右正眼 Migi Seigan

防備ノ構

平一文字

抱囲ノ構

防備構 Bobi Kamae	平一文字 Hira Ichimonji	抱囲ノ構 Hoko no Kamae

此五ツノ構ヲ五法ノ位取リト云フ〒一図ノ右正眼ハ普通直立ノ次姿勢カラ左足ヲ右側前

カラ右側ニ踏ミ開イタ形デ右足ヲ延シテ丁度X字形ニ足ヲブツ・チガヘタ形ニシ

テ右手五指ヲ立テ相手方ノ方へ突キ出シ左拳ヲ胸ニ〒ニ抱圍ニ備ヘタル形也左

正眼ハ右正眼ノ反対ノ姿勢ヲ取ル・此次姿勢ハ始メハ〒行イニクイガ練習デア

ル・十文字ハ相手方ノ隙ヲ見出シテ拳又ハ指頭ヲ出ス体勢也・抱圍ノ構ハ腰

ヲ落シ両手ヲ頭部ノ高サニ開イテ相手ノ周圍ヲ此姿勢デ廻リ隙ヲ見テ両

足・両手飛込ミ当込ムノ次姿勢也・防備ノ構ハ平然トシテ相手方ニ何ノ敵意

モ無イ自然無想トモ云フ可キ構ニテ柔カク指ニモ力ヲ入レザル形也

此五つの構を五法の位取りと云う。第一図の右正眼は普通、直立の姿勢から左足を右側前から右側に踏み開いた形で右足を越して丁度Ｘ字形に足をぶっちがえた形にして右手五指を立て、相手方の方へ、突き出し、左拳を胸に第二の抱囲に備えたる形也。左正眼は右正眼の反対の姿勢を取る。此姿勢は、始めは一寸行いにくいが、練習である。平一文字は相手方の隙を見出して拳又は指頭を出す体勢也。抱囲の構は腰を落し、両手を頭部の高さに開いて相手の周囲を此姿勢で廻り、隙を見て両足、両手飛込み当込むの姿勢也。防備の構は平然として相手方に何の敵意も無い自然夢想とも云う可き構にて柔かく指にも力を入れざる形也。

ちょっと

These five stances are known as the *Goho no Guraidori*, or The five ways of positioning yourself.

	Illustration one shows **Migi Seigan.** This position starts from a regular standing positon. The left foot is in front on the right hand side thereby opening up the body. This is achieved by stepping past the right foot with your left so that you have made an X shape with your legs and your feet have been reversed. The five fingers of the right hand should be extended with the tips stabbing toward the opponent. The left hand is on the chest, ready to shift into the Hoko Kamae shown in the second illustration.
	Hidari Seigan Hidari Seigan is the opposite of Migi Seigan. Incidentally, this stance will feel awkward at first but continue to practice.
	Hira Ichimonji The feeling of Hira Ichimonji is to seek out gaps in the opponent's defense and strike with either the fist or the fingertips.
	Hoko no Kamae When taking Hoko no Kamae drop your hips and raise your hands level with your head. The feeling here is circling your opponent in an open stance. When you find an opening jump in and strike with both feet or both hands.
	Bobi no Kamae Bobi no Kamae is a stance that seems as if you are standing naturally. The opponent should not detect any threat from you. You should be relaxed with no power in even your fingers. The body should stand naturally and anyone looking at you would think you are in a dream-like state.

一、平素ノ練習方法

道場ノ柱ニ人体ノ太サ長サ程度ノ藁ヲ巻キ其上ニ布ヲ固ク巻イテ拳
指先、足先ヲ練ヘル練習ヲスル凡ソ首、胸、下紋ト思ハレル処ニ印ヲ付ケテ
練習ヲスル事

練習目黙視表

主トシテ拇指〇、拇指先ト拇指関節、人差指ト中指、無名指ノ三指五指
五本ノ指先全部ヲ中間ニシテ用フ、面部、足ノ膝頭、次ニ足指、足ノ甲(カ
ト)等モ用フ、手ノ指先ハ主トシテ拇指、此拇指先ヲ用フル時ハ拳ニシテ拇指
先ヲ突出シテ用フ、拇指関節ヲ用フル時ハ拳ニシテ拇指関
節ヲ用フ、一指、二指、三指ヲ用フル時ハ始メ、五指共立テ、相手方ニ向フ
扱テ打込ム場合ニ其手ヲ半開キト変化シテ其急所ヲ掴ムガ如キ心持チニ
テ当込ム、半開キハ〇此如クニシテ一指、二指、三指ヲ用フル也、拳ヲ用フル
場合ハ拇指ヲ中ニ折込マズ外側ニ折ル仁王拳ト云フ四指ノ関節ヲ並ベテ
用フ可ベシ、〇上図ノ如シ、面部ニ用フル場合ハマツ毛ヨリ二寸上部ニ用フ

平素の練習方法

道場の柱に人体の太さ長さ程度の藁を巻き、其上に布を固く巻いて拳、指先、足先を錬える練習をする。凡そ首、胴、下段と思われる処に印を付けて練習をする事。

Typical Training Methodology

Wrap rice straw, Wara, around a column in the dojo until it is approximately as thick as a person's body. Over that firmly wrap a piece of cloth. Use this to strengthen your punches, fingertips and toes. Mart the target to indicate where the neck, body and lower strikes should land. Make sure you draw on the target roughly where the neck, body and lower body strikes should go.

練習黙視表

主として  拇指  拇指先と拇指関節、人差指と中指、無名指の三指、五指、五本の指先全部を中開きにして用う。面部、足の膝頭、次に足指、足の甲（カ、ト）等も用う。手の指先は主として拇指、此の拇指先を用うる時は拳にして拇指先を突出して用う。  拇指関節を用うる時は  拳にして拇指関節を用。一指、二指、三指を用うる時は始めは  五指共立て、相手方に向う。扨て打込む場合其手を半開きと変化して其急所を摑むが如き心持ちにて当込む。半開きは  此如くにして一指、二指、三指を用うる也。拳を用うる場合は拇指を中に折込まず外側に折る仁王拳と云う四指の関節を並べて用う可べし。  上図の如し。面部に用うる場合はまつ毛より一寸上部に用う。

Visual Training Regimen Guide

	Primarily, thumb strikes are either Boshi-saki, a strike with the end of the thumb,
	Or Boshi-Kansetsu, with the joint of the thumb.

The Hitosashi Yubi, Nakayubi and Munayubi, or index finger, middle finger and ring finger, can be used together. When using all 5 fingers, keep your hand half-open and the strike with the fingertips. Strikes with the forehead and kneecaps are used in addition to kicks with the toes and heel.

	The finger most frequently used is the thumb. The way to do this is to make a fist and extend your thumb, stabbing the end forward.
	When striking with the knuckle of the thumb make a fist like this.
	When striking with one, two or three fingers first extend your arm with all 5 fingers pointing at the enemy. As your hand closes in to strike, close your hand half-way. This means you are ready to grab the Kyusho, vital point.
	Here is an image of what half-way open should look like. You use the first three fingers.
	When striking with your fist, do not wrap your thumb inside your fingers, instead it should be on the outside, with the knuckles of your other four fingers in alignment. This is known as Nioken, or "fist of the Kongo-rikishi" that stand guard in front of temples. This is shown in the illustration. When striking to the face aim for a spot 1 Sun, 3cm, above the eyelashes.

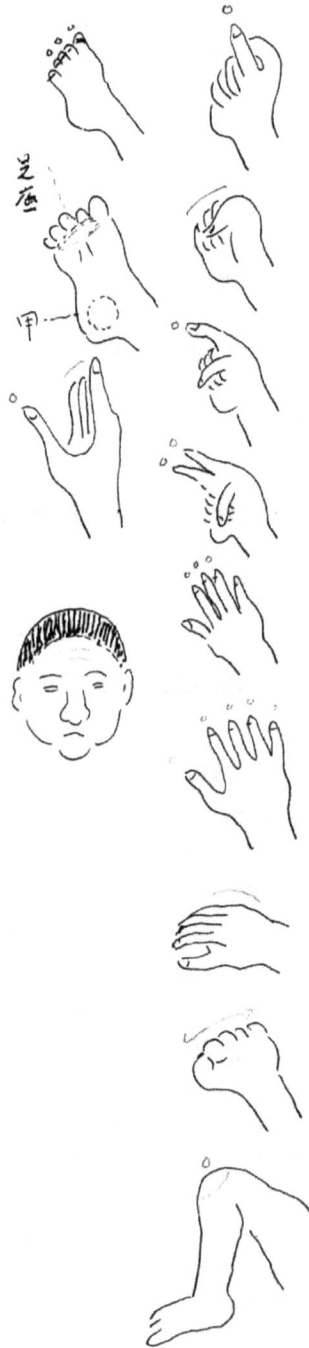

足ハ膝頭ヨリ下段（金的）ヲ主トス脂ノ甲ハ下段、朝霞、攫、攫扼、時ノ当込ミニ用フ足ノ甲（カ、ト）ハ九元、水月、面部ニ用フ、藁人形ニ対シ練習ハ足ノ蹴込ミニ体モ元ニ返スコトシ指先ハ其技ニ対シ指固メ形ハ形ニシテ急ガズ清ク正シク補ル事ニ於テ技ヲ成ス練習シヲコタル可カラズ、形ノ練習ノ場合ハ炎身ハ炎胴シ当テ実地当込ミシ用フ．

骨法術ニ主トシテ使用スル四天八光十二形ト称スルモーセ

足は膝頭にて下段（金的）を主とす。指の甲は下段、朝霞、攉、攉、扼、時の当込みに用う。足の甲（か、と）は九穴、水月、面部に用う。藁人形に対し練習は足の蹴込み体も元に返すこなし、指先は其技に対し指固め形は形にして急がず清く正しく捕る事に於て技を成す練習をおこたる可からず。形の練習の場合は受身は皮胴を当て実地当込みを用う。

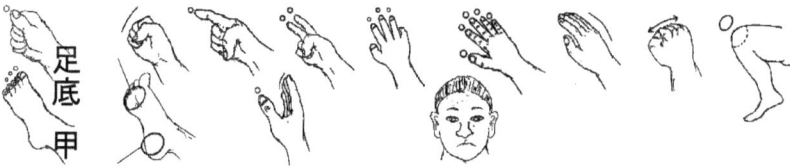

足底
甲

骨法術に主として使用する四天八光十二形と称するもの也。

For the most part the knees are used to strike to Gedan, lower targets, like Kinteki the "Golden Target," or the groin. The knuckles of the fingers are used on lower targets as well as Asagasumi, Sai, Kaku, Yaku and Toki. Kakato, the heel of the foot, is used to strike to Kyu-ana, Suigetsu and Menbu.

When using a Wara Ningyo, or straw practice doll, the force of your kick should not cause you to lose your balance. It is important when training the fingers that you keep an image of the technique you are doing in your mind. It is better to do the technique cleanly and correctly than to rush. This is how you should train. When training Kata, you should practice realistically striking the skin and body of your training partner.

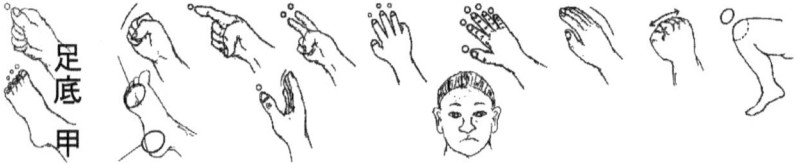

骨法術に主として使用する四天八光十二形と称するもの也。

These are the 12 ways of striking used in Koppo Jutsu.
These are called the Four Heavens and Eight Lights.

Bottom of the foot	
Heel	

初伝

Shoden

Initial Stage Techniques

一、柳（ヤナギ）　投（トウ）　初傳

右がけ　右がけ　平一文字ノ摎

左がけ　左技ノ事　以下仝じ

（愛）ハ左袖左胸ヲ捕リニ来ル（飯）ハ此手ノ秋デ夕雲ヲ捫

指先デ（右手ノ）突上ゲルト仝時ニ右足ニテ発方ノ右足ヲ大外ノ

如ク掛ケテ投ゲル

初伝

一　　抑投　　右がけ　　　平一文字の構
　　　よくとう　左がけ

　　右がけ　　（受）は片袖、左胸を捕りに来る。（取）は此
　　　　　　　手の形で夕霞を拇指先で（右手の）突上げると同
　　　　　　　時に右足にて受方の右足を大外の如く掛けて投げ
　　　　　　　る。
　　左がけ　　左技の事、以下同じ

Shoden : Initial Stage
Yokuto : Suppress and Throw
Left and right sides from Hira Ichi Monji Kamae

Right side: The opponent approaches and grabs your right sleeve
and left lapel. Respond by striking up to Yugasumi with the end of
your thumb. At the same time use your right leg to do a hooking
sweep to the outside of the opponent's right leg and throw.
The left side is done the same way, but on the opposite side.

Hira Ichimonji no Kame	Yugasumi: the depression behind the ear
Boshiken	Boshiken

26

左
がけ

ハユ・ぃ

右が
サ

虎
ハユ

ハユ

(二)
押（オウ）

虎（ギャク）

ハユ

ハユ

（受ハ右腰扱ゲヲ充分ニ掛ケル（前ハ）右手ハ直ケニ放シ後方へ廻ハス気持チニテ左手拇指先ヲセ扱ニグット差込ム（蛇練羽白ハセ

扱ニ左拇指ガ一寸当テル大ケニスベレ）

事実ニ於テハ拇指ヲ差込ム時ハセ日间腰立タズ注意

二　押虐　<ruby>押虐<rt>おうぎゃく</rt></ruby>　同同同　　　　同

右がけ　（受）は右腰投げを充分に掛ける。（取）は右手
　　　　は直ちに放し、後方へ廻す気持ちにて左手拇指先
　　　　を七抜にぐっと差込む（此練習は七抜に左拇指が
　　　　一寸当てる丈けにすべし）。
　　　　事実に於ては拇指を差込む時は七日間腰立たず。
　　　　注意
左がけ　同じ

Shoden : Initial Stage # 2
Ohgyaku : Shove and Punish
Left and right sides from Hira Ichi Monji Kamae

Right side: The Uke moves in and attempts a strong hip throw. You
respond by yanking your right arm back and twisting your body
backwards at the same time. Use the thumb of your left hand to push
firmly into Shichi-batsu. (For training the goal is to just to locate
and press slightly on Shichi-batsu.) If you were to push in hard
enough with your thumb it would result in the opponent not being
able to stand for seven days. It is therefore important to be cautious.
The left side is done the same way, but on the opposite side.

Hira Ichimonji no Kame	Shichi-batsu is located on the back above the hipbone

（三）杭柳　コウ　ヨウ　人ニ　人ニ

右　ガ　ケ　人ニ

左　ガ　ケ　人ニ　ジ

（受）ハ右拳ニテ面部ニ打込ミ来ル（取）ハ左腕ニテ左ニ受ケ直チニ右拳ニテ表鬼門ニ当込ミ仝時ニ左腕ヲ受方ノ右手ノ脇下ヨリ右肩ノ方ニ廻シ左腰ヲ入レ背負投ゲ
ノ方ニ廻シ左腰ヲ入レ背負投ゲ

三　抗抑 _{こうよく}　　　同

右がけ　（受）は右拳にて面部に打込み来る。（取）は左
　　　　腕にて受け直ちに右拳にて表鬼門に当込み同時に
　　　　左腕を受方の右手の脇下より右肩の方に廻し左腰
　　　　を入れ背負投げ
左がけ　同じ

Shoden : Initial Stage # 3
Kohyoku : Flatten Resistance
Left and right sides from Hira Ichi Monji Kamae

Right side: The opponent punches to your face. Block this with
your left arm and immediately punch to Omote Kimon, the Front
Devil's Gate. At the same time bring your left hand under the
opponent's right armpit and over onto the right shoulder. Enter with
the left side of your hip and throw the opponent over your back.
The left side is done the same way, but on the opposite side.

Hira Ichimonji no Kame	Omote Kimon the Front Devil's Gate are all the points in the half circle above the nipple

四　指[さ]　倒[トウ]　仝　仝

右がけ　仝

（受）ハ両胸ヲ捕リニ来ル（取）ハ直チニ右手拇指ヲ関節シ

左がけ　仝

上図ノ如キ形ニテ霞返シニ当テ左足ヲ退キ体ヲ捻ネル
敵ハ倒レル

九

四　指倒 _{しとう}　同　　　　同
　　　　　　　同

　右がけ　（受）は両胸を捕りに来る。（取）は直ちに右手
　　　　　拇指〔〕関節を上図の如き形にて霞返しに当て左
　　　　　足を退き体を捻ねる。敵は倒れる。
　左がけ　同じ

Shoden : Initial Stage # 4
Shitoh : To Topple With the Fingers
Left and right sides from Hira Ichi Monji Kamae

Right side: The opponent grabs both lapels. You immediately press

the knuckle of your right thumb 〔〕 to Kasumi Gaeshi,
Returning Mist. Draw your left foot back and twist your body. This
should cause the opponent to fall.
The left side is done the same way, but on the opposite side.

Hira Ichimonji no Kame	Kasumi Gaeshi "Returning Mist" Located 2 Sun, 6 centimeters, below the ear.
	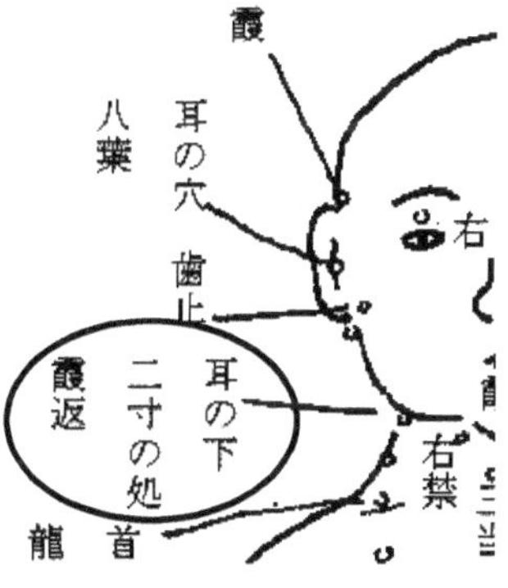

㈤　捕捉ハ　防備之構

右がけ　（受）ハ左手ニテ胸ヲ持チ右拳ニテ打込ム　（取）ハ左腕ニテ受

方ノ右拳ヲ受ケ　右手拇指ニテ声ニ当入リ面部ニテ

左がけ　受方ノ顔面ヲ打ツ　人ニじ

五　捕捉 ^{ほそく} 同同　　　防備之構

右がけ　　（受）は左手にて胸を持ち右拳にて打込む。（取）
　　　　　は左腕にて受方の右拳を受け、右手拇指にて声に
　　　　　当入り面部にて受方の顔面を打つ。
左がけ　　同じ

Shoden : Initial Stage # 5
Hosoku : To Restrain
Left and right sides from Bobi no Kamae

Right: The opponent grabs your right lapel with their left hand and
punches with their right. You should block this right punch with
your left arm. Strike with the thumb of your right hand to the point
known as Koe, and head-butt the opponent in the face.
The left side is done the same way, but on the opposite side.

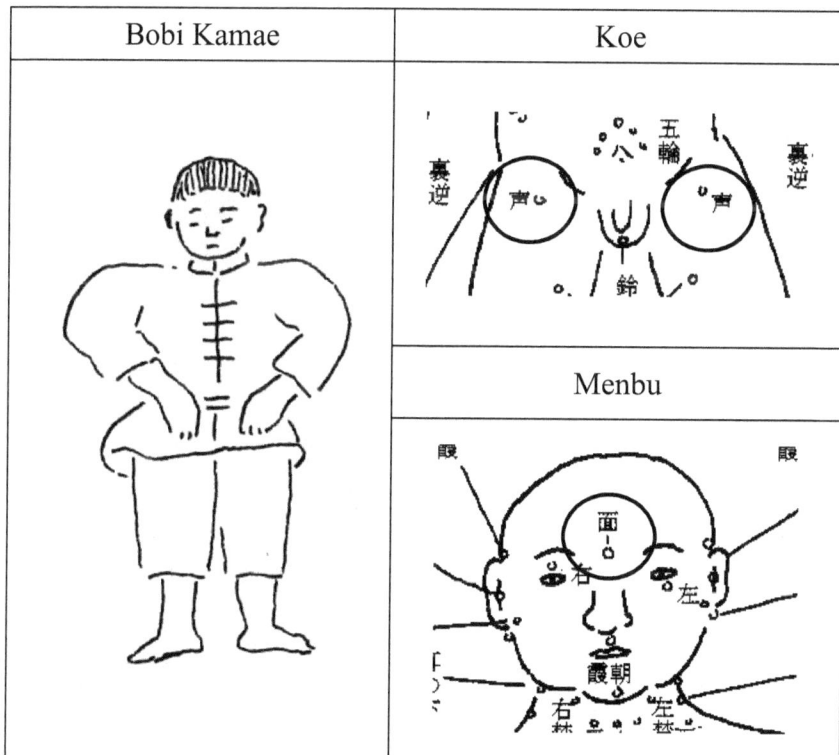

Bobi Kamae	Koe
	Menbu

左
が
け 合ニ

右
が
け 合ニ 合ニ

(六)
放ホゥ 擲テキ 合ニ 合ニ

（受）ハ左手ニテ胸ヲ持チ右拳ニテ打込ミ来ル（取）ハ左手刀

ニテ受方ノ右手ノ星ヲ跳ネ上ゲ右ノ手ハ敵ノ左手星ニ

拇指ヲ当テ掴ミテ上部ニ押シ上ゲ右腰ヲ入レテ

投ゲル

六　放擲　<ruby>ほうてき</ruby>　同
　　　　　　　　　　　同
　　　　　　　　　　　同　　　　　同

右がけ　　（受）は左手にて胸を持ち右拳にて打込み来る。
　　　　　　（取）は左手刀にて受方の右手の星を跳ね上げ、
　　　　　　右手は敵の左手星に拇指を当て掴みて上部に押し
　　　　　　上げ右腰を入れて投げる。
　　　左がけ　　同じ

Shoden : Initial Stage # 6
Hoteki : Throw Out
Left and right sides from Bobi no Kamae

Right: The opponent grabs your right lapel with their left hand and
punches with their right. With left hand strike upward with a Shuto
to Hoshi. Use the thumb of your right hand to press into the left
Hoshi of the opponent. Next push the opponent's left arm up, and
move your right hip in and throw.
The left side is done the same way, but on the opposite side.

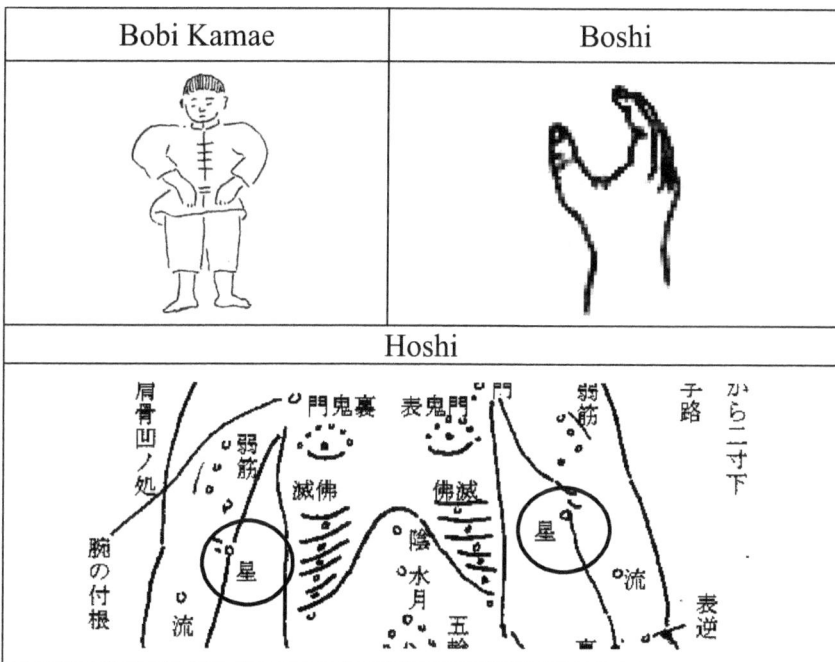

Bobi Kamae	Boshi
Hoshi	

（七）斜倒[シャトウ]　仝ヒ

右かけ　仝ヒ　仝

左かけ

（受）左手ニテ胸ヲ持チ右拳ニテ打込ミ来ル（扨）ハ左手ニテ受方ノ右拳ヲ受ケ右手ノ拇指ヲタ霞ヲ打ット仝時ニ膝頭ニテ敵ノ鈴ヲ蹴上ゲテ倒ス　仝ニ

七　斜倒　^{しゃとう}　同同　　　同

右がけ　（受）左手にて胸を持ち右拳にて打込み来る。（取）
　　　　は左手にて受方の右拳を受け右手の拇指を夕霞を
　　　　打つと同時に膝頭にて敵の鈴を蹴上げて倒す。
左がけ　同じ

Shoden : Initial Stage # 7
Shatoh : Diagonal Throw Down
Left and right sides from Bobi no Kamae

Right: The opponent grabs your right lapel with their left hand and
punches with their right. Receive the opponent's right punch with
your left arm. Strike to Yugasumi with the thumb of your right hand
and, at the same time, strike upwards to Suzu, the bell, with your
kneecap. This will cause the opponent to fall.
The left side is done the same way, but on the opposite side.

Bobi Kamae	Boshi
Yu Gasumi "Night Mist"	Suzu "Bell"

（ハ）掛ケ　倒（タオシ）　人ェ　人ェ

右がけ　人ェ　人ェ

左がけ　人ェ　じ

（芝）ハ両胸ヲ捕リニ来ル（取）ハ左右ノ手ヲ拳ニシテ敵ノ表逆

ヲ打チ払ヒ右足ヲ一歩退ク其ノ退イタ反動ニテ全時ニ敵ノ五

輪ヲ右足ノ甲（カヒト）ニテ蹴リ倒ス

八　掛倒^{かけたおし}　同同　　　同
（Note: hand-written ruby above 掛倒 reads かけたおし; to the right are 同同 and 同）

右がけ　（受）は両胸を捕りに来る。（取）は左右の手を拳
　　　　にして敵の表逆を打ち払い右足を一歩退く。其の
　　　　退いた反動にて同時に敵の五輪を右足の甲（かゝ
　　　　と）にて蹴り倒す。
左がけ　同じ

Shoden : Initial Stage #8
Kaketaoshi : Attack and Topple
Left and right sides from Bobi no Kamae

Right: The opponent grabs both lapels. Strike downward with both
the left and right hands to the outside or inside of the opponent's
hands as you step back with your right foot. Use the motion of
dropping back to kick the opponent in Gorin with the Kakato, or
heel, of your right foot. This will cause him to fall down.
The left side is done the same way, but on the opposite side..

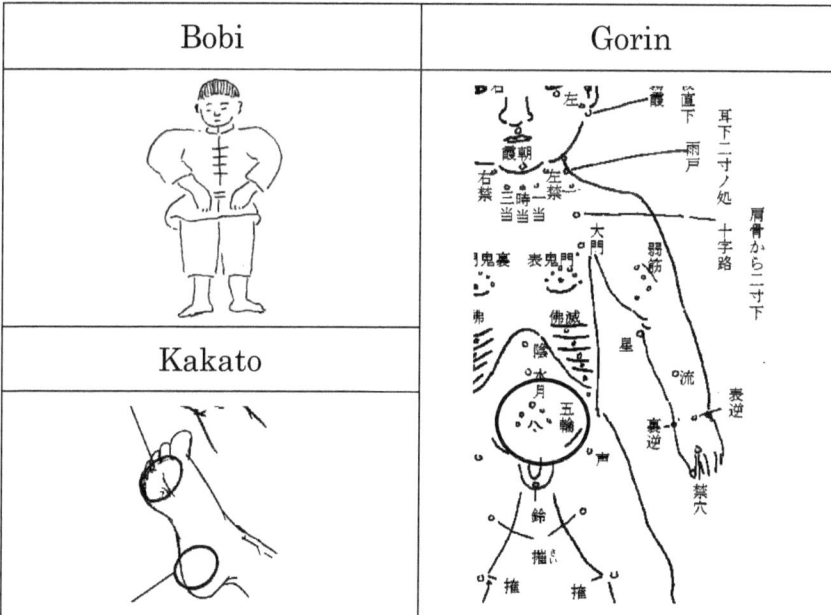

Bobi	Gorin
Kakato	

（九）搾撃（サクゲキ）手　人ユ　人ユ

人ユ

右がけ
（受ハ両胸ヲ捕リニ来ル（取）ハ右　拇指ガ敵ノ頸ノ裏（朝霞）
二掛ケ上ニ押上ゲ右ヲ甲ニ搾ヲ横ニ就リ倒ス

左がけ　人エ…じ

41

九　搾撃 さくげき 同 同　　　同

右がけ　（受）は両胸を捕りに来る。（取）は右拇指が敵
　　　　の顎の裏（朝霞）に掛け上に押上げ右足甲にて摧かく
　　　　を横に蹴り倒す。
左がけ　同じ

Shoden : Initial Stage #9
Sakugeki : Twist and Attack
Left and right sides from Bobi no Kamae

Right: The opponent grabs both your lapels. Shove the thumb of
your right hand behind the jaw (to Kasumi) and lift up. Do a side
kick to Kaku with your right heel to topple the opponent.
The left side is done the same way, but on the opposite side.

Bobi Kamae	Boshi
Asa Gasumi "Morning Mist"	Kaku

㈣　撍タ゛キ　ゲキ　人ニ

右ガけ　敵手ゲキ　人ニ

左ガけ　人ニじ

（炭）ハ両拳ニテ打込ミ来ル（飯）ハ一才腰ヲ井落シ両手稍上ニ揚ゲル之ニハ虚也実ハ右之甲ニテ水月ヲ蹴リ倒ス

十　憺撃　同 同　　　同

右がけ　（受）は両拳にて打込み来る。（取）は一寸腰を落
　　　　し両手稍上に揚げる。之れは虚也。実は右足甲に
　　　　て水月を蹴り倒す。
左がけ　同じ

Shoden : Initial Stage # 10
Tangeki : Quiet Attack
Left and right sides from Bobi no Kamae

Right: The opponent punches right. Drop your hips slightly and raise both hands slightly, this is a Kyo, or feint, a lie. Your real response, Jitsu, is to do a heel kick to Suigetsu, the solar plexus.
The left side is done the same way, but on the opposite side.

Bobi Kamae	Suigetsu

（二）抜技（ヌキワザ）

右ガケ　人ニ　人ヌ

（受）ハ右手ヲ胸ヲ捕ル（取）ハ其ノ右手ノ表ニ我ガ左手拇指ノ剣（此ノ関節ヲ用ヒテ掴ミ左上部ヘ逆ニ掛ケルト人ニ時ニ

左ガケ　人ニジ

右手五指先ニ受方ノ左横面ノ左ト人トニ当込ニ倒ス

十一 抜技 ばつ ぎ　同
同　　　同

右がけ　（受）は右手にて胸を捕る。（取）は其右手の表逆
　　　　に我が左手拇指の⟨図⟩此の関節を用いて掴み、左
　　　　上部へ逆に掛けると同時に右手五指先にて受方の
　　　　左横面の左と人とに当込み倒す。
左がけ　同じ

Shoden : Initial Stage # 11
Baggi : Pulling Out Technique
Left and right sides from Bobi no Kamae

Right: The opponent grabs your chest with their right hand. Take
Omote Gyaku wrist lock with your left hand. Use the thumb to press
into the joints on the back of the hand as you raise it up. At the same
time strike with your right hand in Goshiken to the left side of the
opponent's face. This should cause the opponent to topple.
The left side is done the same way, but on the opposite side.

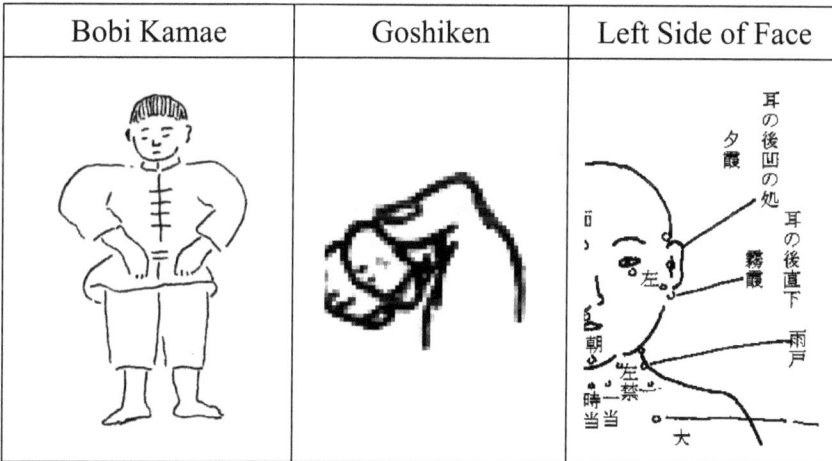

Bobi Kamae	Goshiken	Left Side of Face

両挬倒（トゥ）　人ニ

右がけ　人ニ

（受）ハ右手ニテ胸ヲ捕ル（取）ハ仝時ニ右拳ニテ受方ノ右手ノ弱筋ヲ右方ヘ打込ムト左手ノ拇指ヲ佛滅ヘ打込ムト仝時

左がけ　セ人ニ じ

十二　折倒 ^{同同}　　　同

<ruby>折倒<rt>せっとう</rt></ruby>

右がけ　（受）は右手にて胸を捕る。（取）は同時に右拳に
　　　　て受方の右手の弱筋を右方へ打込むのと左手の拇
　　　　指を仏滅へ打込むのと同時也。
左がけ　同じ

Shoden : Initial Stage # 12
Settoh : Break and Topple
Left and right sides from Bobi no Kamae

Right: The opponent grabs your lapel with their right hand. The
moment the hand grabs your lapel strike to right Jakkin with your
right fist.   At the same time strike with your thumb into the
opponent's Butsumetsu.
The left side is done the same way, but on the opposite side.

Bobi Kamae	Butsumetsu
	Jakkin

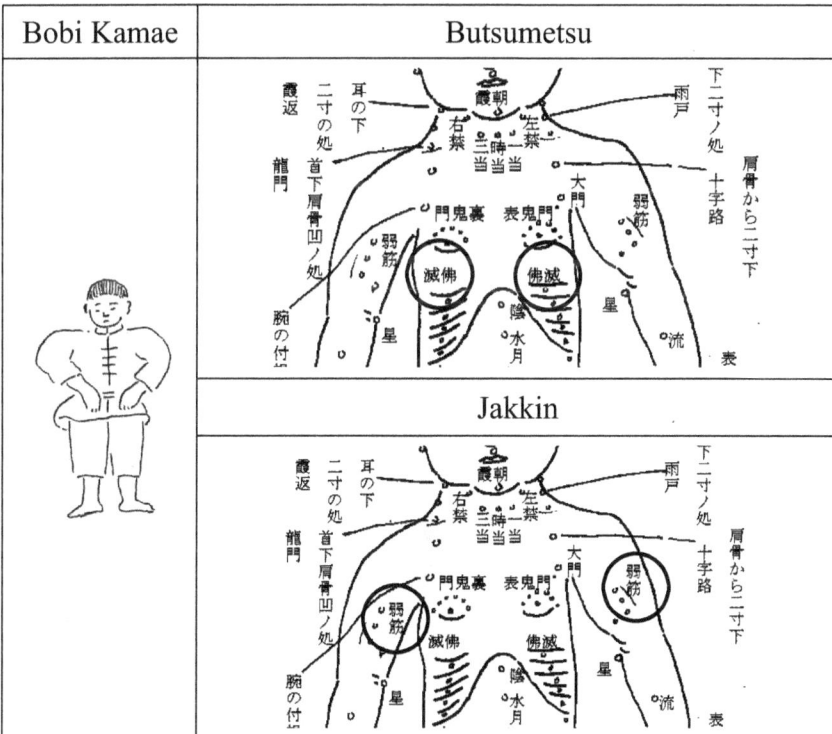

48

面指し 拍リ 人ス

右がけ 人ス

左がけ 人ス

（変）ハ両拳ヲ打込ミ来ル（取）ハ右足ヲ右後方ヘ大キク下ル

ト仝時ニ右足ヲ鈴ニ蹴込マントスル虚ニシテ実ハ右拳

ヲ陰ニ当込ミ倒ス

人ス

十三　指拍　<ruby>指拍<rt>しはく</rt></ruby>　同同　　同

右がけ　　（受）は両手にて打込み来る。（取）は右足を右後
　　　　　方へ大きく下ると同時に右足を鈴に蹴込まんとす
　　　　　る虚にして実は右拳を陰に当込み倒す。
左がけ　　同じ

Shoden : Initial Stage # 13
Shihaku : Finger Beat
Left and right sides from Bobi no Kamae

Right: The opponent punches first right then left. Respond by
dropping a big step back and right with your right leg. As soon as
you do this feint like you are going to kick to Suzu with your right
foot. This is Kyo the lie. The Jitsu, or true intent, is punching with
your right fist into Kage and toppling the opponent.
The left side is done the same way, but on the opposite side..

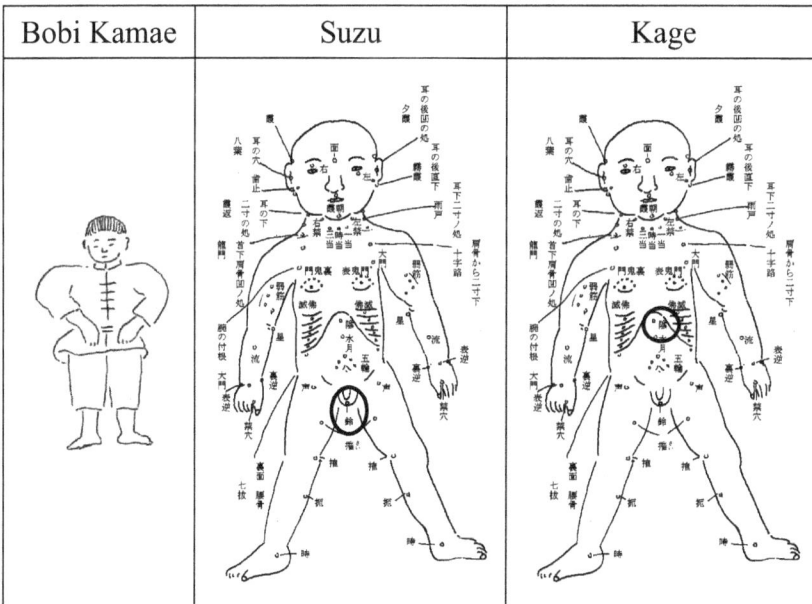

Bobi Kamae	Suzu	Kage

両
拒技ぎ　人ユ

右がけ　人ユ
（受ハ両拳ニテ打込ミ来ル（販ハ右足ヲシ右後方ヘ大キク下ルト仝時ニ右足ヲ時ヲ蹴付ケルト仝時ニ右拳ヲ陰ニ当込ム（此ノ時ト

左がけ　人ユ
云フハ足ノ内側俗ニ梅干ト云フ処ノ二寸前上部也）

十四 拒技　<ruby>拒技<rt>きょぎ</rt></ruby>　同同同　同

右がけ　（受）は両拳にて打込み来る。（取）は右足を右後
　　　　方へ大きく下ると同時に右足にて時を蹴付けると
　　　　同時に右拳を陰に当込む（此の時と云うのは足の
　　　　内側、俗に梅干と云う処の一寸前上部也）。
左がけ　同じ

Shoden : Initial Stage # 14
Gyogi : Resistance Technique
Left and right sides from Bobi no Kamae

Right: The opponent comes in with a right punch then a left punch.
Respond to this by taking a big step back and to the right with your
right foot. Immediately kick to Toki and strike to Kage with a right
punch. (This spot known as Toki is on the inside of the foot. It is
slightly above the point known colloquially as Umeboshi.)
The left side is done the same way, but on the opposite side.

Bobi Kamae	Toki	Kage

高　捌_{カッ}捊_{コウ}　人ニ

右ガケ　人ニ

（受）ハ両拳ヲ打込ミ来ル（取）ハ右足ヲ右後方ニ一歩退クト同時ニ敵ノ右足ヲ攫ヲ右足甲ニテ蹴込ミ右手ノ三指ニテ一当・時ノ当

左ガケ　人ニ

三当リヲ以テ突倒ス

53

十五 括拷 <ruby>かつこう</ruby> 同 同　　　　同

右がけ　（受）は両拳にて打込み来る。（取）は右足を右後
　　　　方に一歩退くと同時に敵の右足擢を右足甲にて蹴
　　　　込み右手の三指にて一当、時の当、三当りを突倒
　　　　す。
左がけ　同じ

Shoden : Initial Stage # 15
Kakkoh : Tie up and Torture
Left and right sides from Bobi no Kamae

Right: The opponent comes in with a right punch then a left punch.
Respond to this by taking a step back and to the right with your right
foot. Immediately kick the opponent in Sai with your right heel.
Strike with the first three fingers to Itto, Toki no Ate and Santo. This
will topple the opponent.
The left side is done the same way, but on the opposite side.

Bobi Kamae	Sai	Itto (1) Toki no Ate (2) Santo (3)

両浦（ウラ）波（ナミ）　仝ユ

右がけ　仝ユ

（笑）両拳ニテ打込ミ来ル（裏）ハ両腕ニテ受ゲ入込ンデ右足ニ敵ノ右足ヲ掛ケ蹴返シ両手拇指一時ニ雨戸ニ打込ム

左がけ　仝ユ　じ

十六　浦波　^同
　　　　　^同　　　同

右がけ（受）両拳にて打込み来る。（取）両腕にて受け入込
んで右足にて敵の右足扼を蹴返し両手拇指一時に雨戸に打込
む。
左がけ同じ

Shoden : Initial Stage # 16
Uranami : Reversing the Wave
Left and right sides from Bobi no Kamae

Right: The opponent comes in with a right punch then a left punch.
Respond by entering in with a two-armed block. Knock away the
opponent's right leg by kicking to Yaku with your right foot. Finally,
strike simultaneously with both thumbs to the left and right Amedo.
The left side is done the same way, but on the opposite side.

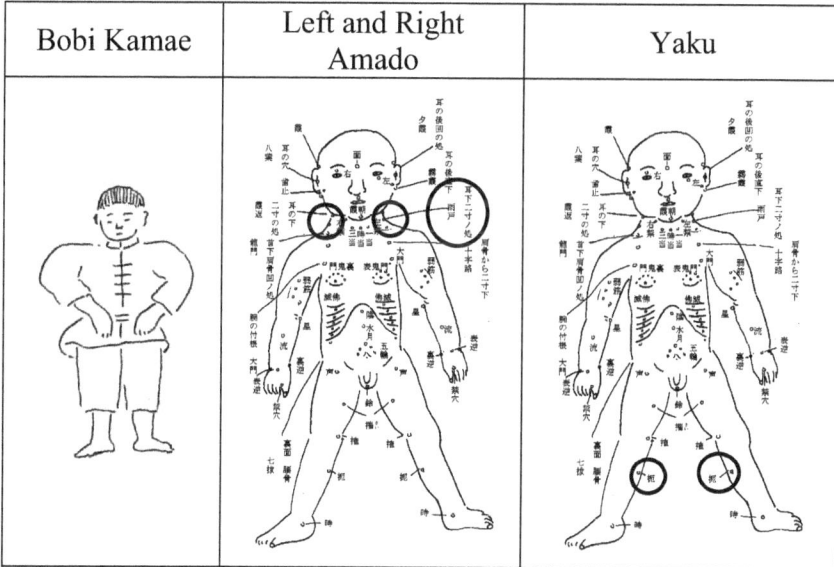

Bobi Kamae	Left and Right Amado	Yaku

志 天（アマ）地（ツチ） 人ヱ

右ガけ（笑）ハ両拳ニテ打込ミ来ル（返）ハ右ヱリ後方ニ退キ仝時ニ右ヱ
指先ニテ鈴ヲ蹴上ゲルート右手五指ニテ左ト人ニ当込ム

左ガけ 人ヱじ
ト仝時ヘ右ガけノ時ハ左、左ガけノ時ハ右ト人ニ当込ム

十七　天地　<ruby>あまつち</ruby>　同
同
同

右がけ　（受）は両拳にて打込み来る。（取）は右足を後方
　　　　に退き同時に右足指先にて鈴を蹴上げるのと右手
　　　　五指にて左と人に当込むのと同時（右がけの時は
　　　　左、左がけの時は右と人に当込む）。
左がけ　同じ

Shoden : Initial Stage # 17
Amatsuchi : Sacred Ground
Left and right sides from Bobi no Kamae

Right: The opponent comes in with a right punch then a left punch.
Respond by stepping back with your right leg and then immediately
kicking with the toes of the right leg to Suzu, the bells. Strike with
Goshi, all five fingers of the right hand, to Left Amado and Jinchu.
(When done on the right side strike Jinchu and Left when doing the
left side strike Jinchu and Right.)
The left side is done the same way, but on the opposite side.

Bobi	Suzu	Left Amado and Jinchu (when using right hand)
Goshi		Right Amado and Jinchu (when using left hand)

両片巻　人ニ

（受）ハ両拳ヲ打込ミ来ル（取）ハ入込ンデ両手ヲ受ケ止メ右

右がけ　人ニ

手ハ敵ノ腕ヲ外側ヨリ内側ニ巻込ムト仝時ニ左手拇指ニ

テ敵ノ右側佛滅ニ当込ム

左がけ　人ニ　左佛滅ニ当込ム

初伝終

十八　片巻　<ruby>片巻<rt>かたまき</rt></ruby>　同
　　　　　　　　　　同

右がけ　（受）は両拳にて打込み来る。（取）は入込んで両
手にて受け止め右手は敵の腕を外側より内側に巻込むのと同
時に左手拇指にて敵の右側仏滅に当込む。
　　左がけ　同じ　左仏滅に当込む。

Shoden : Initial Stage # 18
Katamaki : Single Wrap
Left and right sides from Bobi no Kamae

Right: Your opponent attacks with a right punch then a left punch.
Respond by blocking both these strikes as they come in. Use your
right arm to wrap up the opponent's arm from the outside to the
inside. At the same time use the Boshi, or thumb, to strike the
opponent in Butsumetsu on the right side.
The left side is done the same way, but on the opposite side. except
you strike left Butsumetsu.

Bobi Kamae	Butsumetsu	Boshi

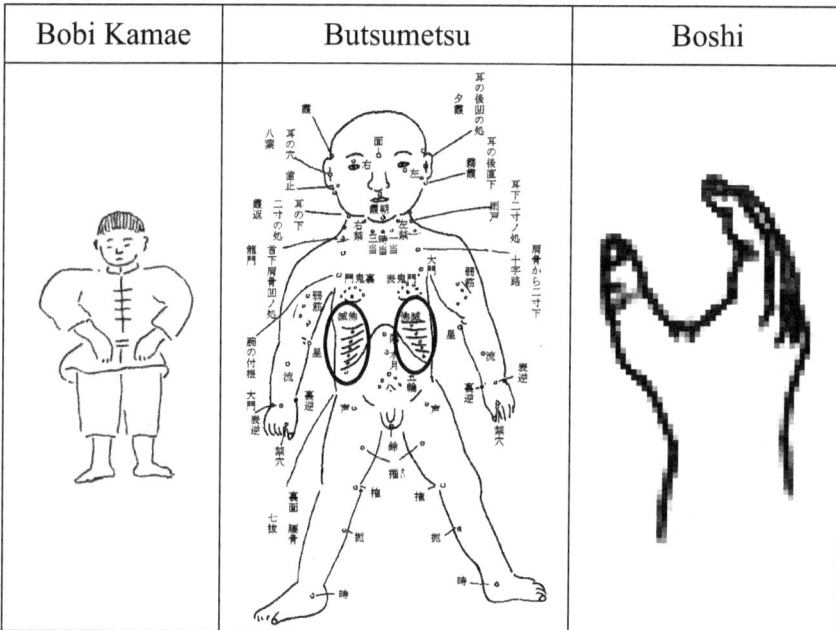

（口伝）

元来骨法術ハ敵ヲ寄セ付ケズ近付ケバ必ズ倒スト云フノデアルガ初段ノ秋ハ不要

ニシテ敵ニ胸ヲ持タセタリ近付ケタトシテノ形ト知ルベシ

敵ノ両戸トカ各当ヲ打タントスル場合始メカラ自分ノ手足・足先ニ力ヲ入レテ

ハナラナイ・技ヲ行フ直前ニ力ヲ入レル事・襟ヲ掴ントシテモ何心ナイト云フ

気分ニシテ襟シツマミ技ヲ掛ケル時ニ拇指ニ力ヲ入レテ一活ニ倒ス

自信ヲ持タネバナラヌ・モシ虚実ヲ行フ時ハ虚ハ如何ニモ此ノ技デ敵

シ倒スゾト勢ヲ見セテ実ハ外ニ技ヲ行フ・之ハ敵ノ心ニ隙ヲ与ヘ

ルノデアル・故々練習ガ重ナルト自然ノ内ニ虚実ガ現ハレ飛込メ

バ必ズ倒ス之レガ骨法術ノ本体デアル

（口伝）

元来骨法術は敵を寄せ付けず、近付けば必ず倒すと云うのであるが、初段の形は不幸にして敵に胸を持たせたり近付けたとしての形と知るべし。敵の雨戸とか各当を打たんとする場合、始めから自分の手足、足先に力を入れてはならない。技を行う直前に力を入れる事、襟を掴としても何心ないと云う気分にて一寸襟をつまみ、扨て技を掛ける時に拇指に力を入れて一活（一括）に倒す自信を持たねばならぬ。もし虚実を行う時は虚は如何にも此の技で敵を倒すぞと勢を見せて実は外に技を行う。之れは敵の心に隙を与えるのである。段々練習が重なると自然の内に虚実が現われ、飛込めば必ず倒す。之れが骨法術の本体である

Kuden

Originally the meaning of the Koppo Jutsu was to keep your distance from your adversary until the moment of attack, which will always topple your opponent. However, understand that, the Shodan, or Initial Level, techniques focus on unfortunate situations that have resulted in your opponent grabbing hold of your chest or otherwise suddenly closing the distance.

When you are moving to attack vital points of the enemy like Uto, 6 cm below the ear, you must not begin with all your power focused in the ends of your hands or feet. Put power in your fingers or toes the moment before you apply the technique. Even if an opponent grabs your collar, it should not disturb your spirit. What should happen is: the opponent grabs your collar, when you are going to apply the technique, all your power must be focused in Boshi, your thumb, and your attack should be one that topples your opponent in one swift motion.

If you are using Kyo-Jitsu, Lie-Truth, then the Lie should appear to your opponent to be full of power and intent, which opens a gap in your opponent's attention so you can apply your intended technique, the Truth.

As you train day after day, you will naturally develop an ability to apply Kyo-Jitsu. If you leap in you will always topple your opponent. This is the fundamental nature of Koppo Jutsu techniques.

中伝
Chuden
Middle Level Techniques

中傳

先ヅ中伝練習ニ先立ッテ飛鳥ノ技ヲ練習スル事ガ肝要デアル。其練習ニハ初メニ素人敵ノ腹部ニ当ル処ニ両足ニテ蹴リ始メハ作向ケニ倒レ背中ヲ道場ノ畳ニ打チツケルデアロウ之ヲ両足ニテ蹴ルト人ハ時ニ両手デ畳ヲ打ッテ一廻転シテ立ッノ練習ニ於テ最後ニハ種々ニ両手指先ガ畳ニ振レル丈ケデ立ッノ事ガ出来ルモノデアル。又柔道ニヨラズドンナ術ヤ道ヲ練習シ又ヨホド練習シテイテモ剛胆ナ人デアッテモ人間ニ誰レモ何カシラ不安ニサソハレル。ウマク技ガ掛ルカ知ラント云フ不安ノ念ニカラレ技ガ出ナイ様ナ事ガ有リ勝デ此時ニ神心ニ依ルノデアル。神心ト云フト何カ迷信的ナ様ニ聞ヘルガ決シテ然ラズ。神心ト云フ事ハ言葉ヲ以テ替ヘルト無念無想トモ言ヘルガ此時相手ハ一ツ人形ニシカ又ハ自信ト強イ確信ヲ持ッテ敵ニ当ル可キデアル。大古ヨリ戦フ前ニ右手ノ人差指ニテ左ノ手掌ニ〈神龍〉ト三度書ク其上戦フ又ト云フ之ヲ神示ト云フテイル。則チ強イ精神ヲ植付ケルガ為メナルヘシ

中伝

先ず中伝練習に先立って飛鳥の技を練習する事が肝要である。其練習には初めは藁人形の腹部に当る処を両足にて蹴り、始めは仰向けに倒れ背中を道場の畳に打ちつけるであろう。之を両足を蹴ると同時に両手で畳を打って一廻転して立つの練習に於て最後には僅かに両手指先が畳に振れる（触れる）丈けで立つ事が出来るものである。又、柔道によらず、どんな術や道を練習し又、よほど練習していても剛胆な人であっても人間は誰しも何かしら不安にさそわれる。

神心と云うと何か迷信的な様に聞えるが、神心に依るのである。神心と云う事は言葉を云い替えると無念無想とも言えるが、此時は神心に依るのである。神心と云う事は言葉を云い替えると無念無想とも言えるが、此時相手は一つの人形にしかずと云う自信と強い確信を持って敵に当る可きである。大古にては、戦う前に右手の人差指にて左手掌に（神龍）と三度書く。其上戦うたと云う。之れを神示と云うている。則ち強い精神を植付けんが為めなる可し。

Chuden : Middle Level Techniques

It is essential to study Hicho no Waza before beginning the Chuden, Middle Level Techniques. The first type of training to do is craft a Wara Ningyo, straw doll shaped like a person, and practice kicking it with both feet at the same time in the abdomen. Initially you will fall flat on your back on the Tatami mats covering the floor of the Dojo. Eventually you will become able to kick with both feet and then land with both arms on the Tatami mats. Using the strike of both arms on the Tatami you will roll backwards and stand up. Eventually your arms will only brush the Tatami mats before you roll backwards and stand up.

Further, regarding Judo or any other martial art one may practice: no matter how much training you do, or how fierce a person may be, a person will always harbor some doubts about themselves. They think, "I don't know if I will be able to apply this technique effectively." This gives rise to an overall lack of confidence in their ability. Some people call it the spirit while others describe it in superstitious terms, none of them amount to much though. What you must do is think of your opponent as nothing more than a doll. You must face your opponent with confidence in yourself and strike with the conviction you will emerge victorious.

There is an old teaching that goes: Before you enter battle extend your right index finger and draw Shin-Ryu 神龍, Dragon-god, three times on the palm of your left hand. After that, fight. This is a kind of divine protection. It should be thought of as something that plants a strong spiritual power in you.

Stroke order for Shin (top) Ryu (middle, below)

何ダカ不思議ナ術ノ現ハレ如ク伝ヘテイルガ実ハ自信デアル・自覚デアル・

虎倒流ノ祖戸田一心斉ヨリ天文筆間百地三太郎ニ伝ヘラレ十一代戸

田大三郎近繁系近デ伊加冥流忍術者ノ秘伝武術トシテ骨法術ト

ヲ行ハレタノデアル・一方凪生判官義鑑房ハ代々義鑑流骨法術トシ

テ広ク伝ヘヲ其子珠ニ伝フ・又鈴木大善大夫近政ハ玉虎流・出雲流骨

法術トシテ伝ヘ・又佐々木源太夫貞安ハ此術ヲ打拳術ニ加ヘ玉心流骨

法打拳術トシテ紀州ニ広ム・又戸田真龍軒ハ本体義鑑流・鎧盤君術・

飛鳥術・虎倒流骨法術トシテ播州方面ニ広ム・神伝不動流体術ヲ高

松先生ノ恩師タリ高松翔翁先生ヨリ上野 貴澄水虎倒流骨法

術ヲ十五代ヲ継承ス・

何だが不思議な術の現われの如く伝えているが、実は自信である。自覚である。
虎倒流租戸田一心斉より天文年間百地三太郎に伝えられし十一代戸田大三郎近繁
迄で伊賀流忍術者の秘伝武術として骨法術を行われたのである。一方、瓜生判官
義鑑房は代々義鑑流骨法術として広く伝えられ、其子孫に伝う。又、鈴木大善太
夫近政は玉虎流、出雲流骨法術として伝え、又佐々木源太夫貞安は此術を打拳術
に加え、玉心流骨法打拳術として紀州に広む。又、戸田真龍軒は本体義鑑流、銛
磐術、飛鳥術、虎倒流骨法術として播州方面に広む。神伝不動流体術、高松先生
の恩師たり。高松翊翁先生より上野貴澄水、虎倒流骨法術第十五代を継承す。

Though this may seem like some sort of mysterious power will manifest itself, in reality it is Jishin, confidence. Jikaku, preparedness.

Toda Issinsai, a revered elder master of Koto Ryu, passed the teachings on to Momochi Santaro in the Tenbun Era. From there it continued to be handed down generation after generation until the 11th successor Toda Daizaburo Chikashige taught the Koppo Jutsu techniques as part of the Hiden Bujutsu, Secret Martial Arts, of the Iga Ryu Ninjutsu practitioners. On another note, Uryu Hangan Gikanbo transmitted Gikan Ryu Koppo Jutsu techniques through successive generations and his descendants taught these techniques widely.

In addition, Suzuki Daizen Tafu Chikamasa passed on the techniques of Gyokko Ryu and Degumo Ryu Koppo Jutsu. Further, Sasaki Gentafu Sadayasu added Dakken Jutsu, Striking Techniques, to these and spread his new Gyokushin Koppo Daken Jutsu in the Kishu area.

Further, Toda Shinryuken Masamitsu learned Hontai "Main Body" Gikan Ryu, Senban Jutsu, Hicho Jutsu and Koto Ryu Koppo Jutsu and spread the teachings in the Banshu area.

Takamatsu Sensei learned Shinden Fudo Ryu Taijutsu from this revered teacher. Takamatsu Gu-o Sensei taught Ueno Chosui Koto Ryu Koppo Jutsu and became the 15 inheritor of the tradition.

一、飛ビ打ガ
右ガケ　左ガケ　右正眼ノ構

右ガケ（甲）ハ我レト相ニ向ハントス（敵）ハ出ントシテ居タ右手ヲ引クト仝時ニ廿落シテ居タ腰ヲ直立シ呉ノ向キガ左ノ向ケ形ニ変化スル此ノ如ク体勢力ハイツデモ此ノ如クデアル始メハ「カニ」ノ横バイノ如ク見苦シイ形デアルガ仝技ヲナ

サントスル場合、又ハ敵ノ攻撃手ヲ変ハサントスル場合イツデモ変化スル体勢デアル此体勢力ハイツデモ此ノ如クナリ飛ビ打ノ場合（甲）ハ我レト相ニ向ハントス（敵）ハ仝時ニ右手刀ニテ敵ノ霞ヲ返シシ打チテ仝時ニ右呉先ニテ鈴ニ掛ケ倒シテ右呉ヲ退キテ残シ

左ガケ
右ガケ
心ノ構トナル
ハ

一　飛打　右がけ　右正眼の構
　　　　ひ だ　左がけ

右がけ　（受）は我れに向わんとす。（取）は出していた右
　　　　手を引くと同時に落していた腰を直立し、足の向
　　　　きが左向けの形に変化する。此の如く体勢はいつ
　　　　でも此如くである。始めは「カニ」の横ばいの如
　　　　く見苦しい形であるが今技をなさんとする場合、
　　　　又は敵の攻撃を変わさん（躱さん）とする場合、
　　　　いつでも変化する体勢である。此体勢はいつでも
　　　　此如くなり。飛打の場合（受）は我れに向わんと
　　　　す。（取）は同時に右手刀にて敵の霞返しを打ち、
　　　　同時に右足先にて鈴に掛け倒して右足を退きて残
　　　　心の構となる。
　　左がけ　同じ

Chuden : Mid-Level Techniques # 1
Hida : Flying Strike
Left and right sides from Migi Seigan Kamae

Right: The opponent makes no effort to attack you. Take his right hand and pull. At the same time straighten up from the stance you have been in with your hips lowered. As you do this switch your stance to a left foot forward stance. This is the stance you should always maintain.

Initially it will seem like a strange stance that causes you to move like a crab however, when you are practicing techniques and the enemy deflects your attack you will be able to adapt yourself easily. You should endeavor to keep this stance.

When doing Hida, the opponent makes no effort to attack. You strike with a right Shuto to Kasumi Gaeshi and kick with the end of your right foot to Suzu. As your opponent falls, pull your right foot back and maintain Zanshin.

The left side is done the same way, but on the opposite side..

Migi Seigan	Kasumi Gaeshi "Returning Mist" Located 6 cm below the ear	Suzu

（二）飛　檄 ^{サク}

右 がけ　人ニ　人ニ

左 がけ　人ニ　じ

（壱）ハ我ニ向ハントス（敵）ハ充分ニ近付ケテ三尺ノ処デ体ヲ立直シ右手拇指先ヲ敵ノ両戸ニ当入レ全時ニ両足ヲ敵ノ胴ヲ挟ミ締メテ全時ニ両手ニテ敵ノ両足ヲキビスヲ引ク敵ハ仰向ケニ倒ル右足ヲ掘リ我ガ右手デ痛メ締メニナス

二　飛搾　ひさく　同同　　　　　同

右がけ　（受）は我れに向わんとす。（取）は充分に近付け
　　　　て三尺の処で体を直立し、右手拇指先を敵の雨戸
　　　　に当入れ、同時に両足にて敵の胴を挟み締めて同
　　　　時に両手にて敵の両足きびすを引く。敵は仰向け
　　　　に倒る。右足扼を我が右手で痛め締めになす。
左がけ　　同じ

Chuden : Mid-Level Techniques # 2
Hida : Flying Squeeze
Left and right sides from Migi Seigan Kamae
Right: The opponent makes no effort to attack. Respond by gradually closing the distance until you are only 3 Shaku, 90 centimeters, apart. Stand up straight and strike to your opponent's Amado with your right Boshi, or thumb. At the same time wrap both your legs around your opponents waist and squeeze. Immediately grab both his Kibisu, or heels, and pull. This will cause the opponent to fall on his back. Apply painful pressure to his right Yaku, calf, with your right hand.
The left side is done the same way, but on the opposite side.

Migi Seigan	Yaku	Amado 6 cm below the ear

（三）飛鶲

人ニ　　人ニ

右ガケ　（受）ハ我レニ向ハントス　（取）ハ前ト人ニジク、右手五指ニテ敵
ノ左ト人ニ当込ミ人ニ時ニ右足ニテ陰ニ蹴込ミ退イテ殘

左ガケ　心ノ構
人ニじ

三　飛鳥^同^同　　　　同

右がけ　（受）は我れに向わんとす。（取）は前と同じく、
　　　　　右手五指にて敵の左と人に当込み、同時に右足に
　　　　　て陰に蹴込み退いて残心の構
　左がけ　同じ

Chuden : Mid-Level Techniques # 3
Hicho : Flying Bird
Left and right sides from Migi Seigan Kamae
Right: The opponent makes no effort to attack. Respond as before
(the same as Hida,) by striking with Goshi, all five fingers into the
opponent's face. You should aim for Hidari, below the left eye, and
Jinchu, center of man. Immediately kick to Kage, the bottom of the
breastbone, and drop back, maintaining Zanshin (state of readiness.)
The left side is done the same way, but on the opposite side.

Migi Seigan	Kage	Hidari and Jinchu (when using right hand)
Goshi		Migi and Jinchu (when using left hand)

（四）飛_ヒ倒_{トウ} 人ヱ 人ヱ

右_{カケ} 人ヱ 人ヱ

左_{カケ} 人ヱ ジ

（芝）ハ赤シニ向ハントス（面）ハ前ト人ヱジ、右手三指ニテ表鬼門ニ
当込ミ其反動ニテ雨足シ以テ敵ノ左右佛滅ヲ蹴込ンデ
雨手畳ヲ叩イテ其反動ニテ元ノ構トナリ残心シナス

四　飛倒　^同　　　　　同
　　ひとう
　　　　　^同

右がけ　（受）は我れに向わんとす。（取）は前と同じ、右
　　　　手三指にて表鬼門に当込み、其反動にて両足を以
　　　　て敵の左右仏滅を蹴込んで両手畳を叩いて其反動
　　　　にて元の構となり、残心をなす。
　　左がけ　　同じ

Chuden : Mid-Level Techniques # 4
Hito : Flying Topple
Left and right sides from Migi Seigan Kamae
Right: The opponent makes no effort to attack. Respond as before
(the same as Hida,) by striking with right Sanshi, Three Fingers, to
Omote Kimon, Outer Devil's Gate. Use the rebound of that strike
to leap up and kick to left and right Butsumetsu. Both hands strike
the tatami and you use that momentum to roll back and return to
Kamae while maintaining Zanshin.
The left side is done the same way, but on the opposite side.

Migi Seigan	Sanshi
Left and Right Butsumetsu	Omote Kimon

（五）
括 カツ
右 がけ

飛 ビ
人ニ
人ニ

（芝）ハ我レニ近付カントス（面）ハ前ト人ニシ、右手刀ニテ敵ノ雨ヲ
打テ左手刀ニテ左ノ雨ニ打込ンデ後ロニ充分飛ビ退キ残

五　　括飛 <ruby>かつぴ</ruby>　同
　　　　　　　同　　　　　　　　同

右がけ　　（受）は我れに近付かんとす。（取）は前と同じ。
　　　　　右手刀にて敵の雨戸を打ち左手刀にて左雨戸に打
　　　　　込んで後ろに充分飛び退き残心の構。
左がけ　　同じ

Chuden : Mid-Level Techniques # 5
Kappi : Bound Flight
Left and right sides from Migi Seigan Kamae
Right: The opponent approaches you. Respond as before (the same as Hida,) by striking the opponent in Amado with a right Shuto, Sword Hand. Immediately strike to the left Amato with a left Shuto. Leap back as far as you can after this strike while maintaining Zanshin.
The left side is done the same way, but on the opposite side.

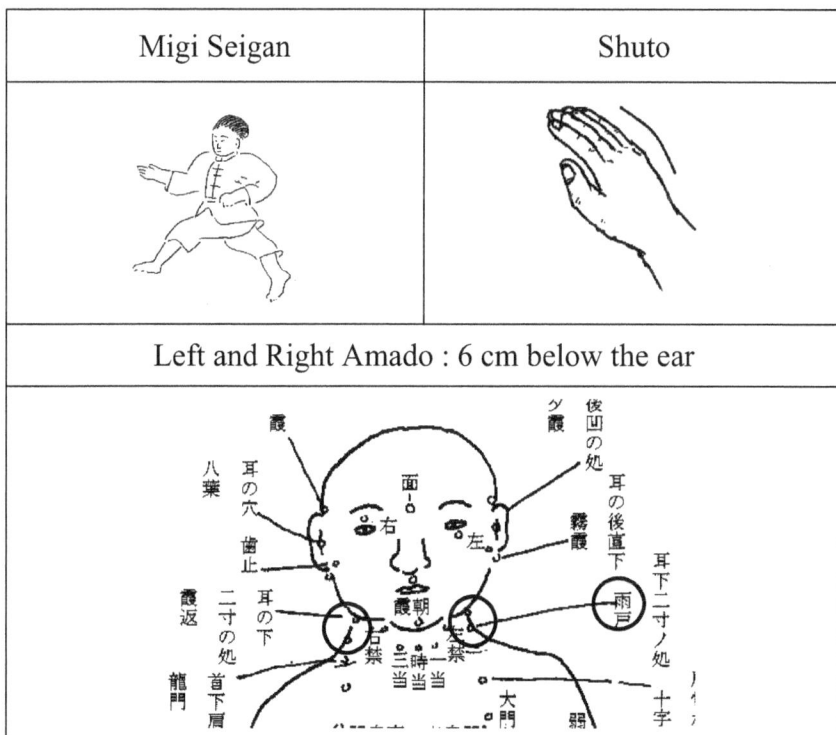

Migi Seigan	Shuto
Left and Right Amado : 6 cm below the ear	

（六）櫚ニ　飛ヒ　人ニ　人ニ

右ガケ　（受）ハネレニ近付キ来ル（取）ハ右手ノ四指ニテ脇ヲ掴ミ拇指ヲ敵ノ伊減ニ当テ捻ネルガ如クニ当入レ全時ニ右足ニテ敵ノ右足ノ

左ガケ　声ヲ蹴倒ス、退イテ残心ノ構　全ジ

六　　押飛　^{同同}　　　　同

もんぴ

右がけ　（受）は我れに近付き来る。（取）は右手の四指に
　　　　て脇を掴み拇指を敵の仏滅に当て捻ねるが如くに
　　　　当入れ、同時に右足にて敵の右足の声を蹴倒す。
　　　　退いて残心の構
左がけ　同じ

Chuden : Mid-Level Techniques # 6
Monpi : Stroking Flight
Left and right sides from Migi Seigan Kamae
Right: The opponent approaches you. Respond by grabbing his
armpit with your right hand. Your first four fingers should grab the
flesh and your thumb should dig into Butsumetsu as you twist.
Immediately kick Koe on his right leg with your right foot, toppling
him. Drop back into Kamae while maintaining Zanshin.
The left side is done the same way, but on the opposite side.

Migi Seigan	All five fingers
Koe	Left and Right Butsumetsu

心（スイ）倒（トウ）人ニ 合

右 かけ 人ニ 合

（受）ハ両拳ニテ打込ミ来ル（取）ハ両手ニテ順ニ受ケ止メ後口ニ飛ビ

退イテ構ヘ、敵再ビ飛込ミ来リ左腕ニテ我ガ首ヲ抱ヘ腰

投ゲニ来ル（取）ハ右肘ニテ敵ノ左傍滅ニ当込ミ其拳ヲ直グ

上ゲ敵ノ人又ハ歯此ニ打込ミ左手ハ敵ノ左首ヲ持ツ手首シ

捕リテ体ヲ完分ニ落シテ右足ヲ敵ノ前ニ出シテ投ゲル

左 かけ 人ニ じ

七　反倒　<ruby>反倒<rt>すいとう</rt></ruby>　同同　　　　　　同

右がけ

（受）は両拳にて打込み来る。（取）は両手にて順に受け止め、後ろに飛び退いて構え、敵再び飛込み来り左腕にて我が首を抱え腰投げに来る。（取）は右肘にて敵の左仏滅に当込み其拳を直ぐ上げ、敵の人又は歯止に打込み左手は敵の左首を持って手首を捕りて体を充分に落して右足を敵の前に出して投げる。

左がけ　　　同じ

Chuden : Mid-Level Techniques # 7
Suito : Flipping Back
Left and right sides from Migi Seigan Kamae
Right: The opponent punches once with each fist. Respond by blocking each with one of your hands, then jump back into Kamae. The opponent jumps in again, wraps his left arm around your neck and attempts to do a Koshi-nage, hip throw. Respond to this attack by striking with your right elbow into the opponent's left Butsumetsu. Then immediately strike upward with the fist of that hand aiming for Jinchu or the area above the teeth. Your left hand should grab your opponent's left wrist and yank it free as you drop your hips down low. Step in front of your opponent with your right foot and throw.
The left side is done the same way, but on the opposite side.

Migi Seigan	Fist	Jinchu	Butsumetsu

左がけ　合ニ

右がけ

（ハ）飄ビョ　合ニ　合ニ

（笑）ハ近付キ来ル（販）ハ右手三指ヲ一当ノ時ノ当ハ三当ノ三ケ所ヲ

指先ヲ下ニ押ス（猫ガ丁度カク如ク）押シ当テ左手五指ノ掌

ヲ上向ケニシテ敵ノ朝霞（顎ノ裏）ヲ当テ右足ヲテ大外ノ如ク

シテ投ゲル　合ニ

八　鼯飛　<ruby>鼯飛<rt>ご び</rt></ruby>　同同　　　　　　同

右がけ　（受）は近付き来る。（取）は右手三指にて一当、
　　　　時の当、三当の三ヶ所を指先にて下に押す（猫が
　　　　丁度かく如く）押し当て左手五指の掌を上向けに
　　　　して敵の朝霞（顎の裏）を当て右足にて大外の如
　　　　くして投げる。
　　左がけ　　同じ

Chuden : Mid-Level Techniques # 8
Kobi : Leap of the Flying Squirrel
Left and right sides from Migi Seigan Kamae

Right: The opponent approaches you. Respond by striking to Itto
(1), Toki no Ate (2) and Santo (3) with three fingers of your right
hand. This resembles how a cat scratches. Push the fingers of your
right hand into these three spots as you strike palm up with Goshiken,
all five fingers of your right hand. You are striking to Asagasumi,
Morning Mist, which is behind the chin.
The left side is done the same way, but on the opposite side.

Migi Seigan	Goshiken	Itto (1) Toki no Ate (2) Santo (3)	Asagasumi "Morning Mist"

（九）

撥ニ 飛 仝 仝 左正眼之構

右かゝけ （受ハ近付キ何モ来ル（取）ハ前ト仝ジク三指ヲ敲ノ当、時ノ当、三当三ケ所シ一時ニ下方ニ押ス、左手五指ニテ敲ノ右ト人ニ突キ当テ右横ニ一間程飛退キ残心ノ構

左かゝけ 之ハ敲ガ後方ニモ有ルト云フ心構也 仝ジ

九　　敝飛　　<ruby>へんぴ</ruby>　同
同

左正眼之構

右がけ　　（受）は近付き来る。（取）は前と同じく三指に
て敵の一当、時ノ当、三当三ヶ所を一時に下方に
押す。左手五指にて敵の右人とに突き当て右横に
一間程飛退き残心の構。

之れは敵が後方にも有ると云う心構也。

左がけ　　同じ

Chuden : Mid-Level Techniques # 9
Henpi : Flying Break
Left and right sides from Hidari Seigan Kamae

Right: The opponent approaches you. Respond by striking to Itto
(1), Toki no Ate (2) and Santo (3) with three fingers of your right
hand. With your left Goshi, or all the fingers of your left hand, strike
to Jinchu and Migi. As soon as you strike leap one Ken, 1.8 meters,
away to your right. Drop back into Kamae while maintaining
Zanshin.

The left side is done the same way, but on the opposite side.

Hidari Seigan	Goshiken	Itto (1) Toki no Ate (2) Santo (3)	Right Amado and Jinchu (when using left hand)

櫟返（テキ）（かへし）　人ゑ　人ゑ

右がけ　人ゑ　人ゑ

左がけ　人ゑ　じ

（愛）ハ近何キ来ル（敵）ハ右手ニ敵ノ左手ヲ「腋下腕ノ方ヘ」テ下ノ処ヲ弱筋ノ一処ヘ右手拇指ヲ当テ四指ニテ腕ヲ掴ム弱筋当テ自然敵ハ腕ヲ上ニ揚ゲル右之甲ニテ敵ノ左搓ヲ蹴込シテ人ゑ時ニ敵ノ左腕ヲ我ガ左腰ノ方ヘ急ニ引下ゲル」此ニテ呼吸ニテ敵ハ前方ニ中返リシテ倒ル

十　　蹴返　てきがえし　同同　同同　　　同

右がけ　　（受）は近付き来る。（取）は右手にて敵の左手
　　　　　「脇下、腕の方へ一寸下の処を弱筋の一の処」へ
　　　　　右手拇指を当て、四指にて腕を掴む弱筋当て、自
　　　　　然、敵は腕を上に揚げる。右足甲にて敵の左摧を
　　　　　蹴込んで同時に敵の左腕を「我が左腰の方へ急に
　　　　　引下げる」此一寸呼吸にて敵は前方に中返りして
　　　　　倒る。
左がけ　　同じ

Chuden : Mid-Level Techniques # 10
Tekigaeshi : Squat and Roll
Left and right sides from Hidari Seigan Kamae

Right: The opponent approaches you. Respond by grabbing the
opponent's right arm at the lower part of Jakkin. Press in with your
right thumb and use the other four fingers to grip the flesh at Jakkin.
This will naturally cause the opponent to raise his arm. Kick with
the top of your left foot to Sai and, at the same time, time pull his
left arm down toward your left hip in a quick motion. This will
cause the opponent to flip over forward in one breath.
The left side is done the same way, but on the opposite side.

Migi Seigan	Sai	Goshiken

（三）

喉倒 仝仝 仝

右がけ　〈突〉ハ近何キ來ル〈飯〉ハ右手三指ヲ敵ノ當・時・當・三當リシ一時ニ押下ゲル仝時ニ拇指ヲ敵ノ右禁ヲ突上ゲテ右足鈴

左がけ…人ヱジ　ヲ蹴倒ス退イテ残心ノ構

十一　喉倉<ruby>こうとう</ruby>　同同　　　　　　同

右がけ　（受）は近付き来る。（取）は右手三指を敵の一当、
　　　　時ノ当、三当りを一時に押下げる。同時に拇指に
　　　　て敵の右禁を突上げて右足、鈴を蹴倒す。退いて
　　　　残心の構
左がけ　同じ

Chuden : Mid-Level Techniques # 11
Kohtoh : Throat Topple
Left and right sides from Hidari Seigan Kamae

Right: The opponent approaches you. Respond by striking the
enemy in Itto, Toki no Ate and Santo with three fingers of your right
hand and push down. At the same time use the thumb of your right
hand to push his collar up. Then kick straight into Suzu, the bells,
with your right foot, toppling him. Drop back into Kamae while
maintaining Zanshin.
The left side is done the same way, but on the opposite side.

Hidari Seigan	Itto (1) Toki no Ate (2) Santo (3)	Suzu "Bell"

三 櫪（カク） 飛（ヒ） 人ユ 人ユ 人ユ

右（がけ）

左（がけ） 人ユじ

（受）ハ近付キ来ル（取）ハ右手ノ拇指ヲ敵ノ右掌ヲ上部ニ突
上ゲルト仝時ニ其ノ手ヲ拳ニシテ朝霞ヲ充分ニ上部ニ突

上ゲルヲハ内股ノ如クシテ突倒ス退テ残心ノ構

中伝終ニ

93

十二　攘飛　<ruby>攘飛<rt>かくひ</rt></ruby>　同同　　　同

右がけ　（受）は近付き来る。（取）は右手の拇指を敵の右
　　　　禁を上部に突上げると同時に其手を拳にして朝霞
　　　　を充分に上部に突上げる。足は内股の如くして突
　　　　倒す。退て残心の構。
左がけ　同じ

Chuden : Mid-Level Techniques # 12
Kakuhi : Flying Abduction
Left and right sides from Hidari Seigan Kamae

Right: The opponent approaches you. Respond by grabbing the his
right collar and pushing up with your right thumb. Push your fist
hard into Asagasumi, Morning Mist, as you lift up. Move your leg
so you can do an Uchi-mata-like throw and topple your opponent
hard. Drop back into Kamae while maintaining Zanshin.
The left side is done the same way, but on the opposite side.

Hidari Seigan	Asa Gasumi "Morning Mist"

たかけ 人ヱし

中伝 終ニ

骨法術ノ指ノ使ニ称ガ肝心デ上部ニ突上ゲル坪ト下部ニ押下ス
坪ニ真直グ当入レル坪 骨盤ヲ掴ムガ如クスル坪トアル事ニ注
意

中伝終

骨法術の指の使い様が肝心で上部に突上げる坪<ruby>坪<rt>つぼ</rt></ruby>と下部に押下す坪、真直ぐ当入れる坪、骨盤を掴むが如くする坪とある事に注意。

End of the Chuden Techniques

The use of the fingers is a fundamental part of Koppo Jutsu. Strikes to upper Tsubo, Vital points, are done upward, while downward force is used when attacking Tsubo on the lower part of the body. Straight strikes are used for the other Tsubo. Pay special attention to Tsubo around the pelvis when grabbing.

奥伝
Okuden
Inner Mysteries Techniques

奥傳

一 攬

当 右がけ 左がけ 自由構

右がけ

（受）ハ飛込ミ来リ扨ガ胸襟ヲ右手ニテ捕リ左手ニテ扨ガ右
袖ヲ掴ミ内股ニ掛ケテ投ゲントス（取）ハ右拳手ヲ敵ノ内股ニ掛
ケテ左足ヲ攫ヒ裏ヨリ上ヨリ叩キ落シ左拳ニテ敵ノ胸ヲ持ツ

左がけ

右腕ノ星シ下ヨリ打上ゲ退イテ残心ノ構
人ニス

奥伝

右がけ
左がけ

一　　<ruby>横当<rt>さんとう</rt></ruby>　　　　　　　自由構

右がけ　（受）は飛込み来り我が胸襟を右手にて捕り、左
　　　　手にて我が右袖を掴み内股に掛けて投げんとす。
　　　　（取）は右拳にて敵の内股に掛けた左足の<ruby>攦<rt>かく</rt></ruby>の裏
　　　　を上より叩き落し、左拳にて敵の胸を持つ右腕の
　　　　星を下より打上げ、退いて残心の構。
左がけ　　同じ

Okuden : Inner Mysteries Techniques # 1
Santoh : Flying Abduction
Left and right sides Jiyu Kamae, Any Kamae

Right: The opponent jumps in and grabs your collar with his right
hand and your right sleeve with his left hand. He then attempts to
throw you with an Uchi-mata. Respond by striking downward into
the back of Kaku on the opponent's left leg, which he is in position
to do Uchi-mata. With your left hand strike upward to Hoshi on the
opponent's right arm, which is holding your collar. Drop back into
Kamae while maintaining Zanshin.
The left side is done the same way, but on the opposite side.

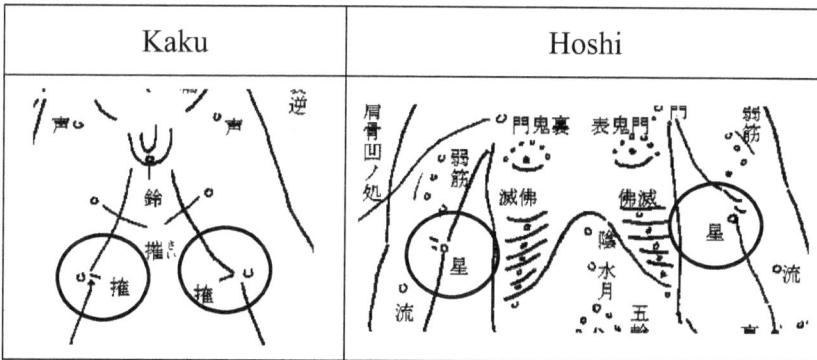

Kaku	Hoshi

（二）攬倒　フヽ

右がけ　フス

（敵ハ小刀ヲ真一文字ニ搆ヘ我ガ胸ニ突込ミ来ル（取）ハ左正眼搆

ヘ左足ニ重身ヲ置キ替ヘ体ヲ退ク丈ケデ敵ノ小刀ハ我ガ左
側ニ流レル・我ガ左手五指ニテ星ヲ突キ仝時ニ左手ニテ敵ノ小
刀ヲ持ッ右手首ヲ掴ミ右足ヲ入込ンデ右拳ニテ敵ノ右表逆
シ内側ニ打ッ敵ノ小刀ハ飛ブ・直チニ右手拙指ヲ敵ノ表逆ニ
当テ持チテ体ヲ右向ケニ変化スル・敵ハ右手ガ逆トナリ伏向
ケトナル左足ヲニテ敵ノ左足ヲ搬ヲ蹴上ゲ突倒ス

左がけ

仝ジ

二　<ruby>横倒<rt>さんとう</rt></ruby>　同
　　　　　　　　　　同

右がけ（受）は小刀を真一文字に構え、我が胸に突込み来
る。（取）は左正眼構え左足に重身（重心）を置き替え、体
を退く丈けで敵の小刀は我が左側に流れる。我が左手五指に
て星を突き、同時に左手にて敵の小刀を持つ右手首を掴み、
右足を入込んで右拳にて敵の右表逆を内側に打つ。敵の小刀
は飛ぶ。直ちに右手拇指を敵の表逆に当て持ちて体を右向け
に変化する。敵は右手が逆となり、伏向けとなる。左足にて
敵の左足摧を蹴上げ突倒す。
左がけ　　同じ

Okuden : Inner Mysteries Techniques # 2
Santoh : Toppling a Forest
Left and right sides Jiyu Kamae, Any Kamae

Right: The opponent is armed with a Shoto, short sword, and is
standing in Shin Ichimonji Kamae. You are standing in Hidari
Seigan Kamae. The opponent stabs at your chest. Shift your weight
to your left foot and drop back one pace so the opponent's short
sword passes your left side. Strike with all five fingers of your left
hand to Hoshi and then immediately grab his right wrist, which is
holding the short sword with your left hand. Step in with your right
foot and punch to the outside of Omote-gyaku. This will send the
enemy's short sword flying. Immediately shift your right thumb so
it is pressing into Omote-gyaku and turn your body to the right. The
enemy's right wrist will now be reversed causing him to start to fall.
Kick up with your left foot to the enemy's left Kaku to knock him
down.
The left side is done the same way, but on the opposite side.

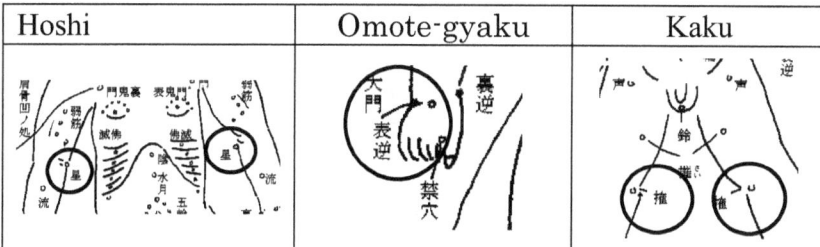

Hoshi	Omote-gyaku	Kaku

三 上 虎倒（トゥ） 人ニ 人ニ

右がけ 人ニ

左がけ 人ニ じ

（受）ハ小刀ヲ大上段ニシテ切込ミ来ル（取）ハ左足ヲ一歩敵ノ右足ノ前ニ飛込ムト仝時ニ左拳ニテ敵ノ右手里ヲ突上ゲ直チニ左右両手同時ニ八葉（頁ノ云）ヲ手掌ニテ打ツ右膝頭ニテ敵ノ鈴ヲ蹴上ゲルト仝時也

三　虎倒<ruby>虎倒<rt>ことう</rt></ruby>　同同

右がけ　（受）は小刀を大上段にして切込み来る。（取）は
　　　　左足を一歩敵の右足の前に飛込むと同時に左拳に
　　　　て敵の右手星を突上げ、直ちに左右両手同時に八
　　　　葉（耳の穴）を手掌にて打つ。右膝頭にて敵の鈴
　　　　を蹴上げると同時也。
　　左がけ　　同じ

Okuden : Inner Mysteries Techniques # 3
Koto : Tiger Felling
Left and right sides Jiyu Kamae, Any Kamae

Right: The opponent is armed with a Shoto, short sword, and is
standing in Daijodan. He cuts down at you. Leap in with your left
foot one step so you are standing in front of his right foot.
Immediately punch upward to his right Hoshi with your left fist, then
immediately do a simultaneous strike with both hands to Happa.
Happa, or Eight Leaves, are the ear canals. Finally, strike upwards
with your right knee to Suzu.
The left side is done the same way, but on the opposite side.

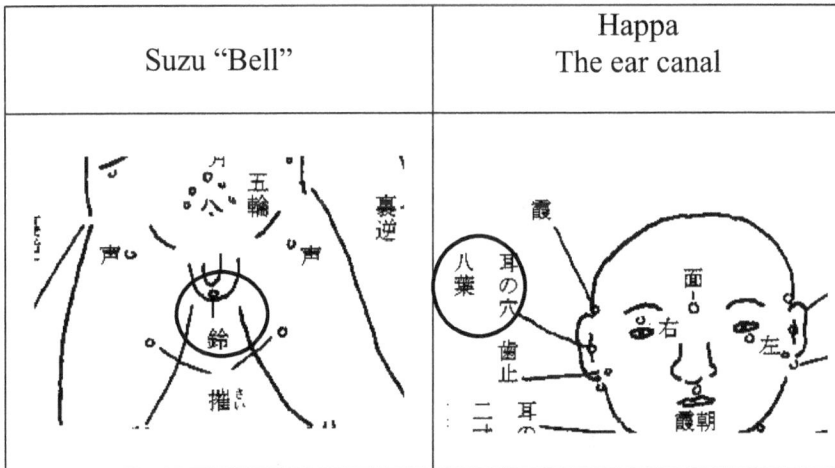

Suzu "Bell"	Happa The ear canal

（四）神剪　人ユ

右がけ　（受）ハ両手ヲ以テ両襟ヲ捕リテ緔メ来ル（取）ハ両手掌ニテ一時ニ敵

ノ左右ノ八葉ヲ打ツノト頭部ニテ敵ノ面ト人ニ打チ付ケル

ト人ユ時也

左がけ　頭部デ頬面ヲ打付ケルカハリニ右手刀ニテ敵ノ右霞ヲ打ツ

テ倒ス

四　　神剪 <ruby>しんせん</ruby>　同同

　右がけ　　（受）は両手にて両襟を捕りて締め来る。（取）
　　　　　　は両手掌にて一時に敵の左右の八葉を打つのと頭
　　　　　　部にて敵の面と人に打ち付けるのと同時也。
　左がけ　　頭部で顔面を打付けるかわりに右手刀にて敵の右
霞を打って倒す。

Okuden : Inner Mysteries Techniques # 4
Shinsen : Heavenly Cut
Left and right sides Jiyu Kamae, Any Kamae

Right: The opponent grabs both of your lapels and begins choking
you. Respond by slapping the palms of your hands against his left
and right Happa, ear canals. Head-butt the opponent in the face and
Jinchu.
Left: Instead of head-butting the opponent, strike to right Kasumi
with a right Shuto, knife-hand.

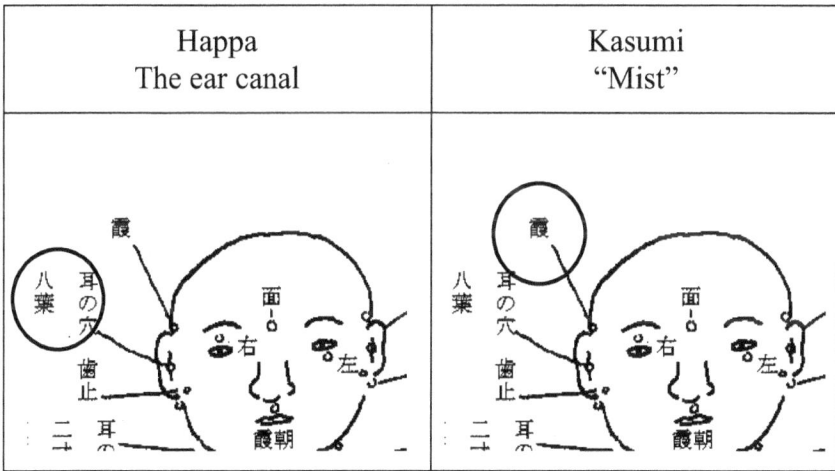

Happa The ear canal	Kasumi "Mist"

四) 楓コシ 飛ビ・ 人ユ 人ユ

右ガケ （受ハ正ニ近付キ来ランドス〈取〉ハ左足ヲ引一歩ノ敵ノ右足前ニ進

左ガケ 人ユ〆 メ左手刀ニテ敵ノ雨戸ヲ打チ・右側ニ飛ンデ残心ノ構

五　　梱飛　<ruby>こんぴ</ruby>　同同

右がけ　　（受）は正に近付き来らんとす。（取）は左足を一
　　　　　歩敵の右足前に進め左手刀にて敵の雨戸を打ち、
　　　　　右側に飛んで残心の構。
左がけ　　同じ

Okuden : Inner Mysteries Techniques # 4
Konpi : Flying in and Wrapping Up
Left and right sides Jiyu Kamae, Any Kamae

Right: The opponent approaches you from the front.　Step toward
the opponent with your left foot, placing it in front of his right foot.
Strike with left Shuto to the opponent's　Amado.　Then jump away
to the right while maintaining Zanshin.
The left side is done the same way, but on the opposite side.

Left and Right Amado

(六)

如(ジョ)手摺(セツ)　仝　仝

右ガケ、(受)ハ近付キ来ル(取)ハ右手ニテ十字路ヲ拇指デ下ニ突キ仝

時ニ体ヲ右斜メニナシテ右足ニテ敵ノ五輪ヲ蹴倒ス

技　右手ヲ使フノト右足ヲ使フノト体ヲ斜メニスルノト三拍子ノ事

左ガケハ仝ジ

六　　　挙摺　<ruby>挙摺<rt>じょせつ</rt></ruby>　同
　　　　　　　　　　　　　　　　　同

右がけ　　（受）は近付き来る。（取）は右手にて十字路を拇
　　　　　指で下に突き同時に体を右斜めになして右足にて
　　　　　敵の五輪を蹴倒す。
技　　　　右手を使うのと右足を使うのと体を斜めにするの
　　　　　と三拍子の事。
左がけ　　同じ

Okuden : Inner Mysteries Techniques # 6
Josetsu : Violent Contact
Left and right sides Jiyu Kamae, Any Kamae

Right: The opponent approaches you. Strike downward onto Jujiro
with Boshi. Immediately twist your body so you are perpendicular
to the opponent and with your right foot kick the attacker in Gorin.
This should knock him down.
Tips for this technique: The use of your right hand, the use of your
right leg and the twisting of your body diagonally are three
important aspects of this techniques and should be done in
succession. The interval between each move should be the same.
The left side is done the same way, but on the opposite side.

Gorin	Jujiro 6 cm below the collarbone

ヒ）抓^{りゃう}

右_{がけ}

掤白^{セツ} 人ェ

人ェ

（釜）ハ近付キ来ル（取）ハ両手三敵ノ両脇ヲ掴ミ拇指両手共両

伸減三当テ体ヲ一テ斜メ三捻ネリ左足ヲ右足ノ後方三笠レ

テ投ゲルヽモ投三拍子ノ事

左_{がけ}

人ェ_じ

七　抓摺　<ruby>抓摺<rt>そうせつ</rt></ruby>　同
　　　　　　　　　　　　同

右がけ　　（受）は近付き来る。（取）は両手にて敵の両脇を
　　　　　掴み拇指両手共両仏滅に当て体を<ruby>一寸<rt>ちょっと</rt></ruby>斜めに捻ね
　　　　　り、左足を右足の後方に坐して投げる。之れも技
　　　　　三拍子の事。
左がけ　　同じ

Okuden : Inner Mysteries Techniques # 7
Sosetsu : Scratching Contact
Left and right sides Jiyu Kamae, Any Kamae

Right: The opponent approaches you. Grab the attacker's armpits
with both hands. As you grip both thumbs should push into
Butsumetsu. Twist your body slightly to the side and pull your left
foot behind your right foot and sit down on it. This will throw the
attacker. These movements are also done Sanbyoshi, meaning while
they are distinct they are done almost simultaneously.
The left side is done the same way, but on the opposite side.

Butsumetsu

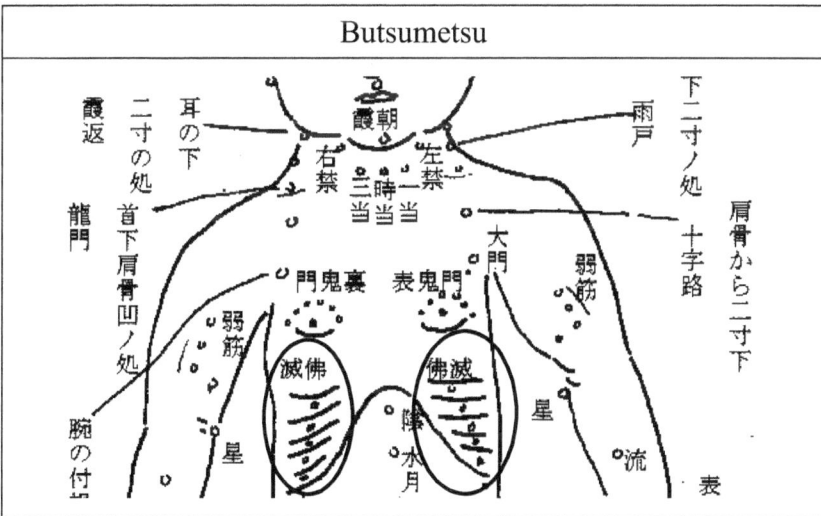

（い）枛倒 トウ 仝

右がけ 仝

左がけ 仝 じ

（変）ハ近付キ来ル（敵）ハ両手ニ敵ノ襟上ヲ掴ミ両手ヲ拊指左

右共禁ニ掛ケ下ニ押シ当テ引イテ我ガ頭部ニテ敵ノ面部ニ

打付ケ右足シ敵ノ声ニ掛ケ車返シ（則チ巴返シ）ニシテ敵ト共

ニ中返リシテ敵ヲ馬乗リトナシ締メル

八　抓倒　<ruby>抓倒<rt>そうとう</rt></ruby>　^同
　　　　　　　　同

右がけ　　（受）は近付き来る。（取）は両手にて敵の襟上を
　　　　　　掴み、両手拇指左右共禁に掛け下に押し当て引い
　　　　　　て我が頭部にて敵の面部に打付け右足を敵の声に
　　　　　　掛け車返し（則ち巴返し）にして敵と共に中返り
　　　　　　して敵を馬乗りとなし締める。
左がけ　　同じ

Okuden : Inner Mysteries Techniques # 8
Soto : Scratching Contact
Left and right sides Jiyu Kamae, Any Kamae

Right: The opponent approaches you. Grab each side of the top of
the attacker's collar with your hands. With your thumbs press into
and downward on left and right Kin. Pull him towards you and
head-butt him in the face. Kick to Koe with your right foot and do
a Kurama Gaeshi, also known as a Tomoe Gaeshi. Stay with the
opponent as you roll so you are mounting him like a horse in the end.
Finish the technique by applying a choke.
The left side is done the same way but on the other side.

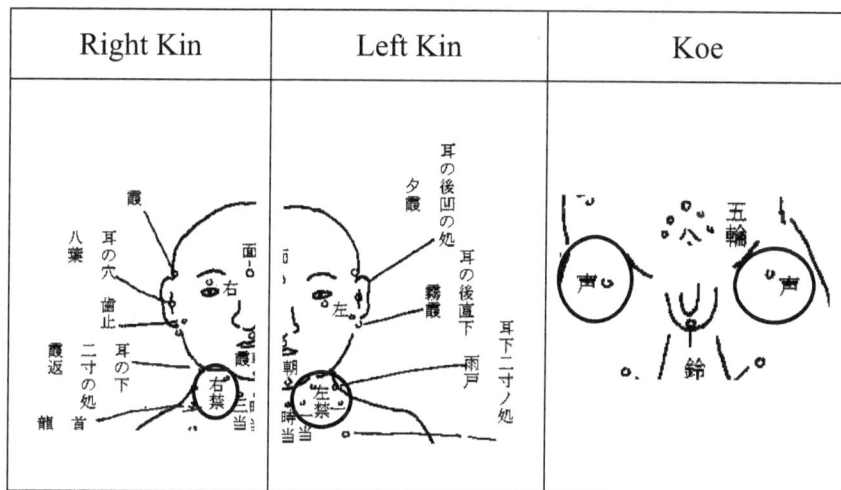

Right Kin	Left Kin	Koe

九 　扣鬼　<ruby>こうき</ruby>　同
　　　　　　　　　　同

右がけ　　（受）は近付き来る。（取）は両手掌にて敵の八葉
　　　　　を左右同時にはたき、両足にて敵の水月を蹴り倒
　　　　　し、其反動にて我れは中返りして元の構となる。
左がけ　　敵近付くなり、我れ両足にて水月を蹴り中返りし
　　　　　て元の構となる。

Okuden : Inner Mysteries Techniques # 9
Kohki : Restraining the Devil
Left and right sides Jiyu Kamae, Any Kamae

Right: The opponent approaches you.　Respond by attacking with
Happa.　The palms of your left and right hands should strike the
opponent at the same time.　Then kick with both feet into Suigetsu.
Use the recoil from that kick to roll back to your starting point and
take Kamae.
Left: As the opponent closes in, kick with both feet to Suigetsu and
use the recoil to roll back to your starting point and take Kamae.

Happa The ear canal	Suigetsu

十　鬼門<ruby>鬼門<rt>きもん</rt></ruby>　同同

右がけ　（受）は近付き来る。（取）は右手で敵の脇下を掴
　　　　み指先で鬼門を押し同時に腰を入れて左足を充分
　　　　に退き坐して投げる。
左がけ　同じ

Okuden : Inner Mysteries Techniques # 10
Kimon : Devil's Gate
Left and right sides Jiyu Kamae, Any Kamae

Right: The opponent approaches you.　Respond grabbing
underneath the opponent's armpit with your right hand.　The tip of
your thumb should dig into Kimon.　Set your hip against his and
then pull your left foot back.　Throw as you sit down.
The left side is done the same way but on attacking Ura Kimon
instead of Omote Kimon.

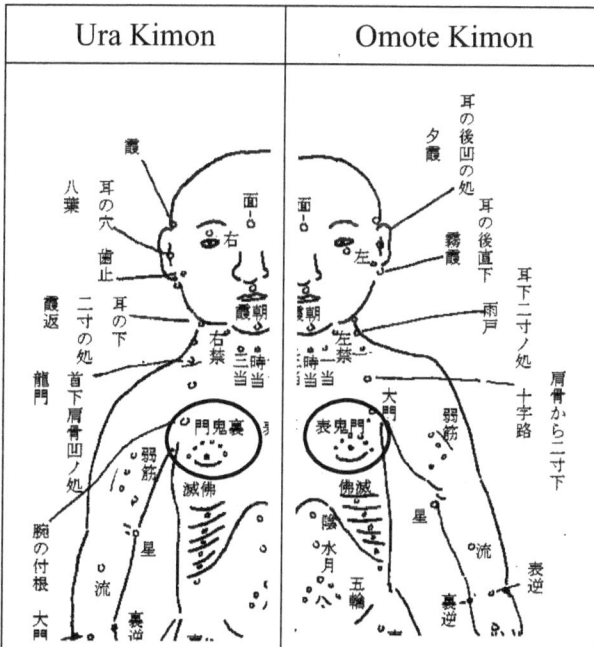

Ura Kimon	Omote Kimon

<ruby>乱<rt>らんせつ</rt></ruby>

十一　乱雪　同
　　　　　　同

右がけ　　（受）は近付き来る。（取）は前と同じく脇下を両
　　　　　手にて掴み、拇指で鬼門を押し、同時に敵の両足
　　　　　の中に我体を流し込む。敵は伏向けに顔面を地上
　　　　　に打つける如く倒る（稽古の時は受方は中返りを
　　　　　なす）。
左がけ　　体を横流しとする事。

Okuden : Inner Mysteries Techniques # 11
Ransetsu : Wild Snowstorm
Left and right sides Jiyu Kamae, Any Kamae

Right: The opponent approaches you.　　Grab underneath both
armpits as in the earlier mentioned technique.
Press into Kimon with your thumbs and, at the same time, slide both
legs between the opponent's legs.　This will cause him to slam his
face into the floor.　When doing training the Uke should do a forward
roll.
Left: Roll to the side.

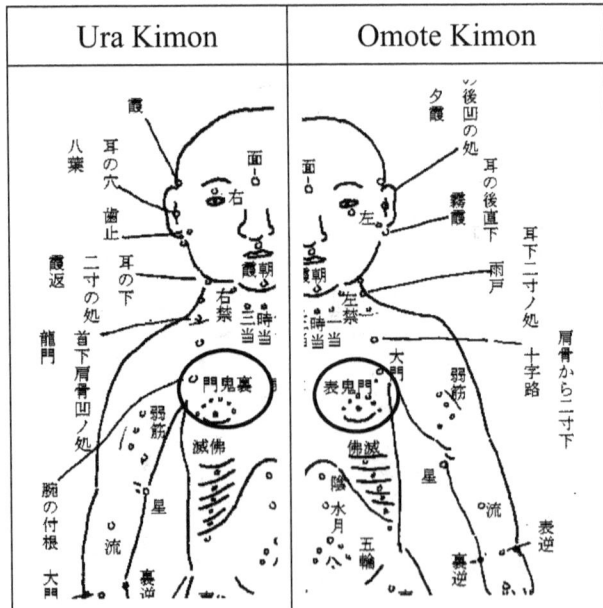

Ura Kimon	Omote Kimon

十二　裏鬼門　<ruby>裏鬼門<rt>うらきもん</rt></ruby>　同
同

　右がけ　　（受）は近付き来る。（我）は右手を上図の如
　　　　　　く乳を掴むが如くにして五指を以て裏鬼門を突き
　　　　　　右足にて五輪を蹴り倒す。
　左がけ　　同じ

奥伝終

Okuden : Inner Mysteries Techniques # 12
Ura Kimon : Reverse Devil's Gate
Left and right sides Jiyu Kamae, Any Kamae

Right: The opponent approaches you.　Grab his breast as shown in

the illustration.　All five fingers should grip Ura Kimon and thrust forward as you knock him down with a right Kick to Gorin. The left side is done the same way but on the other side.
End of the Okuden

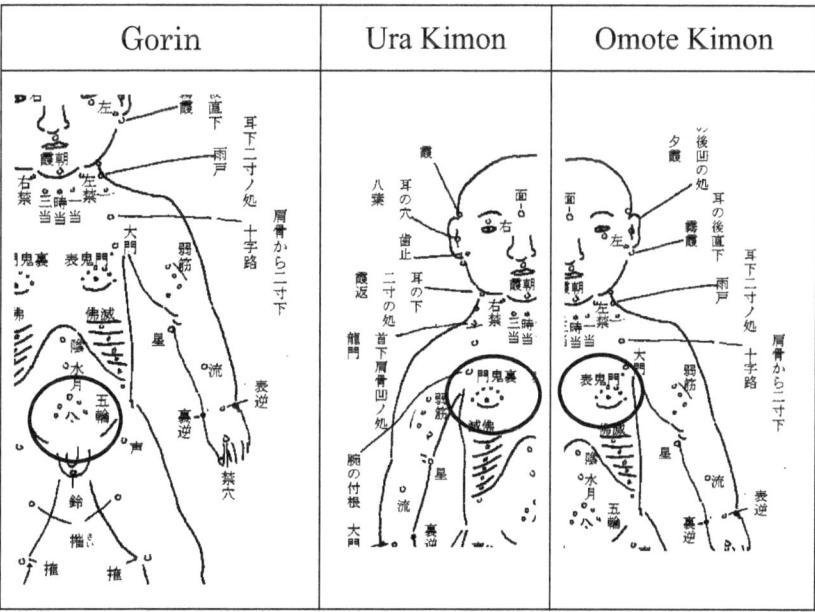

Gorin	Ura Kimon	Omote Kimon

許之傳
Yurushi no Den
Techniques Handed Down to Authorized Students

（一）

佛心

許之傳

許ノ佛心トハ此ノ骨法術ノ本体リ言ヒ表ハセシ事ニシテ
例ヘバ敵ガ近付キ来ル敵ト左手ヲ敵ノ方ニ出シテ居ル時ハ左手
ハ縮メ右手ヲ右横ニ出スト仝時ニ右横ニ飛ビ退ク右手ヲ出シテ
居ル時ハ右手ヲ縮メ左手ヲ横ニ出スト仝時ニ左横ニ飛ビ退
ク後口ニ退ラントスル時ハ一度両手ヲ前ノ地ニ付ケ後ロニ飛ビ
退ク上部ニ飛バントスル時ヲ体ヲ落シ地上ヨリ右手ニテ叩ク気
合ニシテ飛ビ上ル,ツビマル処ヲ敵ヲ痛メズ敵ヲ逃ガルニ
敏捷ナル技ニテ本法ノ骨子ナリ

許之傳

ほとけごころ
一 佛 心

> 許の佛心とは、此の骨法術の本体を云い表わせし事に
> して、例えは敵が近付き来る。我れ左手を敵の方に出
> して居る時は左手は縮め右手を右横に出すと同時に右
> 横に飛び退く。右手を出して居る時は、右手を縮め、
> 左手を左横に出すと同時に左横に飛び退く。後ろに退
> らんとする時は、一度両手を前の地に付け、後ろに飛
> び退く。上部に飛ばんとする時も体を落し、地上を右
> 手にて叩く気分にして飛び上る。つゞまる処、敵を痛
> めず、我れ逃がるゝに敏捷なる技にて本法の骨子なり。

Yurushi no Den
Techniques Handed Down to Authorized Students
Exemption Lesson

One
Hotoke Gokoro : Spirit of the Buddha

This technique called Yurushi no Hotoke Gokoro, Asking
Exemption in the name of the Spirit of the Buddha. It is used when
enemies approach you. If enemy appear on your left, then draw in
your left arm and extend your right arm out to the side, then
immediately jump to the right.

If they attack from the right then draw your right arm in and
extend your left arm out to the side and immediately jump left out
of range.

When retreating backwards, drop down and touch both hands
to the ground before jumping back out of range.

When jumping up, first drop your body down and make as if
striking the ground with your right hand before leaping up.

This method is used when you are surrounded and in a difficult
position. You can use it to escape with deft and quick movement
without injuring your opponents. This is how Hotoke Gokoro is
used.

（二）鬼心

敵四方八方ヨリ来リ或ハ逃ガル、ニ術ナク止ムシ得ズ心シ鬼ニシテ敵ヲ倒スニハ骨法術者ガ常ニ要意セル鍔、鞴石技ゲ（手裏劍）ヲ用ヒ敵ヲ皆倒シ靜カニ退ク

（三）神心

之ニハ敵ヲ一見シテ前知シ精神修養ニ於テ敵ノ精神ヲサクランセシムル事ガアルガ之ニハ高天原宗門之巻ニ属ス

二　鬼心
<small>おにごころ</small>

敵四方八方より来り。我れ逃がるゝに術なく止むを得
ず心を鬼にして敵を倒すには、骨法術者が常に要意
（用意）せる銚磐投げ（手裏剣）を用い、敵を皆倒し、
静かに退く。

Two
Oni Gokoro : Devil's Spirit

Opponents advance on you from all directions and you do not have
any technique that will allow you to escape. In such a situation you
can only adopt the Devil's Spirit and topple your opponents. This
can be done since a Koppo Jutsu Sha, one adept at Koto Ryu striking
arts, always has Senban ready to throw. Senban Shuriken are
employed to attack all your opponents, topple them and allow you
to silently withdraw.

三　神心
<small>かみごころ</small>

之れは敵を一見して前知し、精神修養に於て敵の精神
をさくらんせしむる事があるが、之れは高天原宗門之
巻に属す。

Three
Kami Gokoro : Divine Spirit

Divine Spirit is used when you have determined in an instant your
enemy's mental state. Using your highly developed mental stake
you sew confusion in your enemy. This belongs to Takamagahara
高天原 "Plain of High Heaven" Scroll.[2]

---

[2] The Plain of High Heaven is a Shinto realm, which is the dwelling
place of the Amatsu Kami, heavenly gods. It is connected to the
Earth by a bridge called *Ama-no-uki-hashi* the Floating Bridge of
Heaven.

当込急所 *Atekomi Kyusho*：
Vital Points and Striking Points
古名称 *Konasho*
Old Names For These Points

Points Transcribed into Standard Kanji

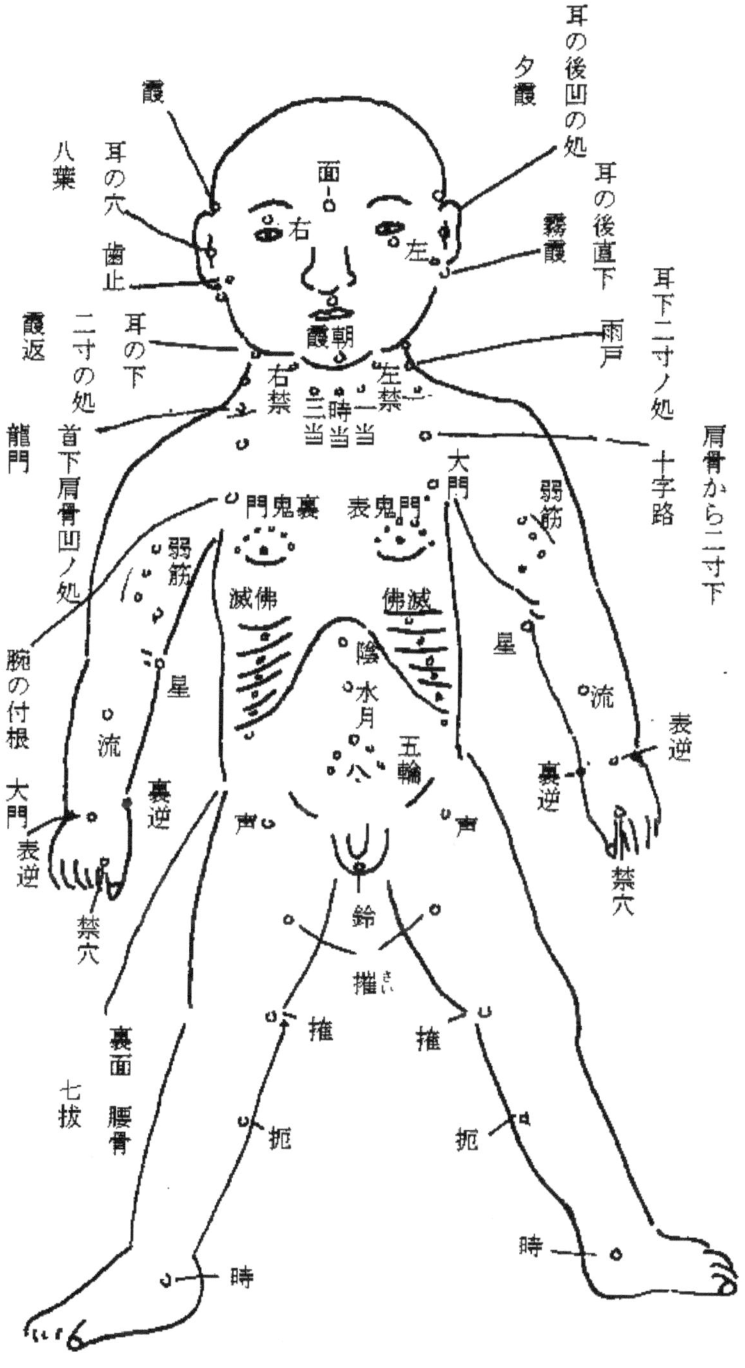

耳の後凹の処
夕霞
耳の後直下
霧霞

霞
八葉
耳の穴
歯止
面
右
左

耳下二寸ノ処
雨戸
十字路
肩骨から二寸下

霞返
龍門
二寸の処
耳の下
首下肩骨凹ノ処
霞朝
右禁
左禁
一時当
二時当
三時当

門鬼裏
表鬼門
大門
弱筋

弱筋
滅佛
佛滅
陰
水月
星
流

腕の付根
大門
表逆
禁穴

星
流
裏逆
五輪
声
声

表逆
裏逆
禁穴

鈴
摧
摧
摧

裏面 腰骨
七抜
扼
扼

時
時

Romanization #1

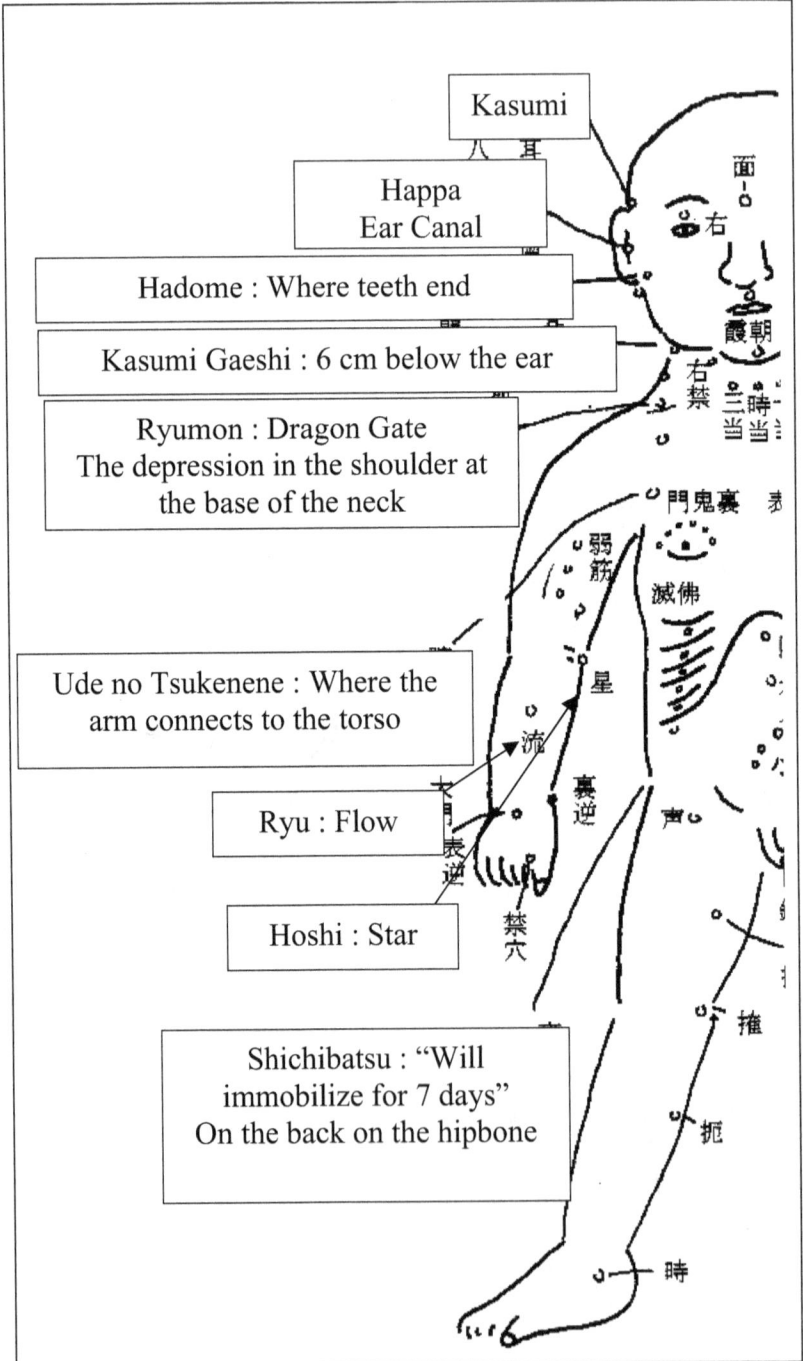

Kasumi

Happa
Ear Canal

Hadome : Where teeth end

Kasumi Gaeshi : 6 cm below the ear

Ryumon : Dragon Gate
The depression in the shoulder at
the base of the neck

Ude no Tsukenene : Where the
arm connects to the torso

Ryu : Flow

Hoshi : Star

Shichibatsu : "Will
immobilize for 7 days"
On the back on the hipbone

八 耳

面

右

霞 朝

右 禁

二 時 一
当 当

門 鬼 裏 表

滅 佛

弱
筋

星

流

大 月
表 裏
逆 逆

裏
逆

声

禁
穴

推

扼

時

Romanization #2

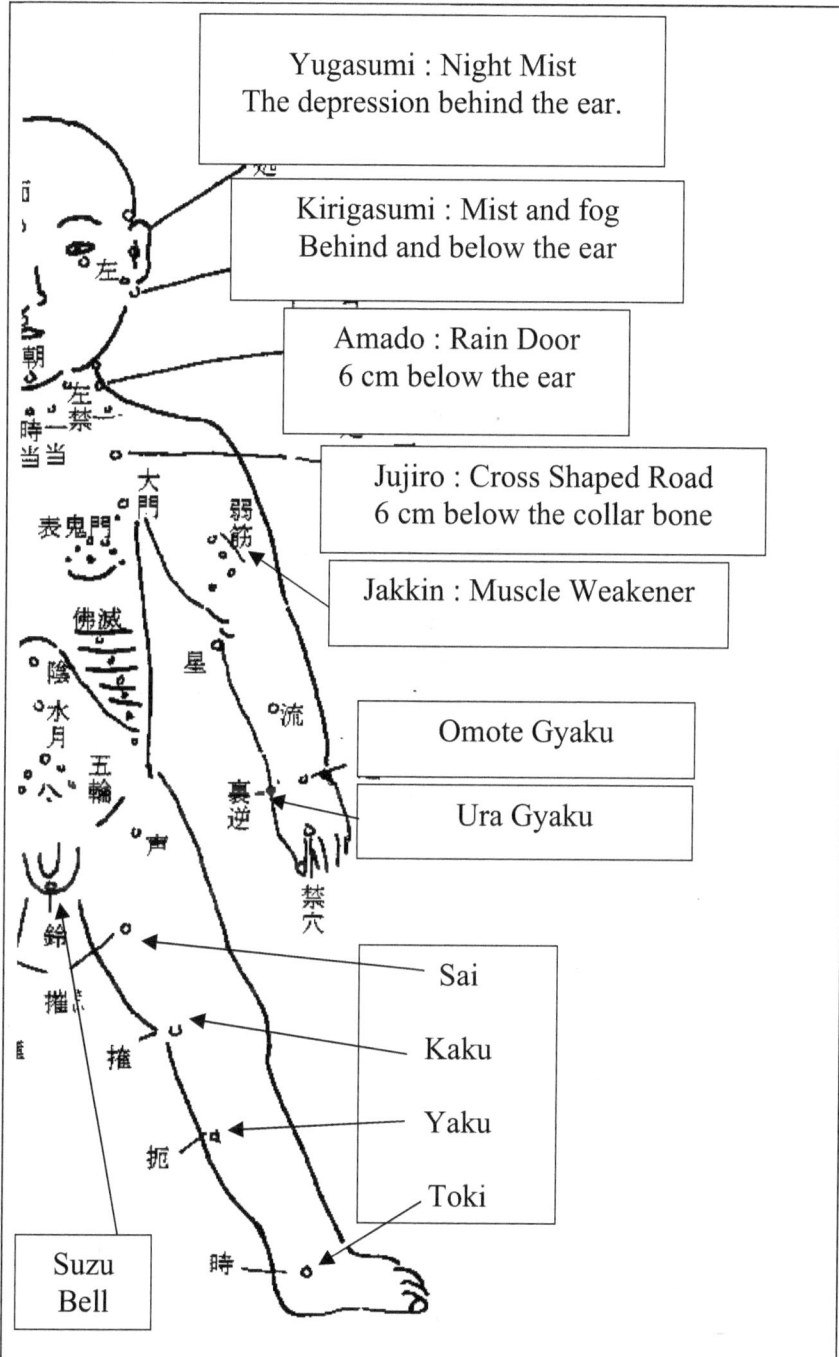

Yugasumi : Night Mist
The depression behind the ear.

Kirigasumi : Mist and fog
Behind and below the ear

Amado : Rain Door
6 cm below the ear

Jujiro : Cross Shaped Road
6 cm below the collar bone

Jakkin : Muscle Weakener

Omote Gyaku

Ura Gyaku

Sai

Kaku

Yaku

Toki

Suzu
Bell

Romanization #3

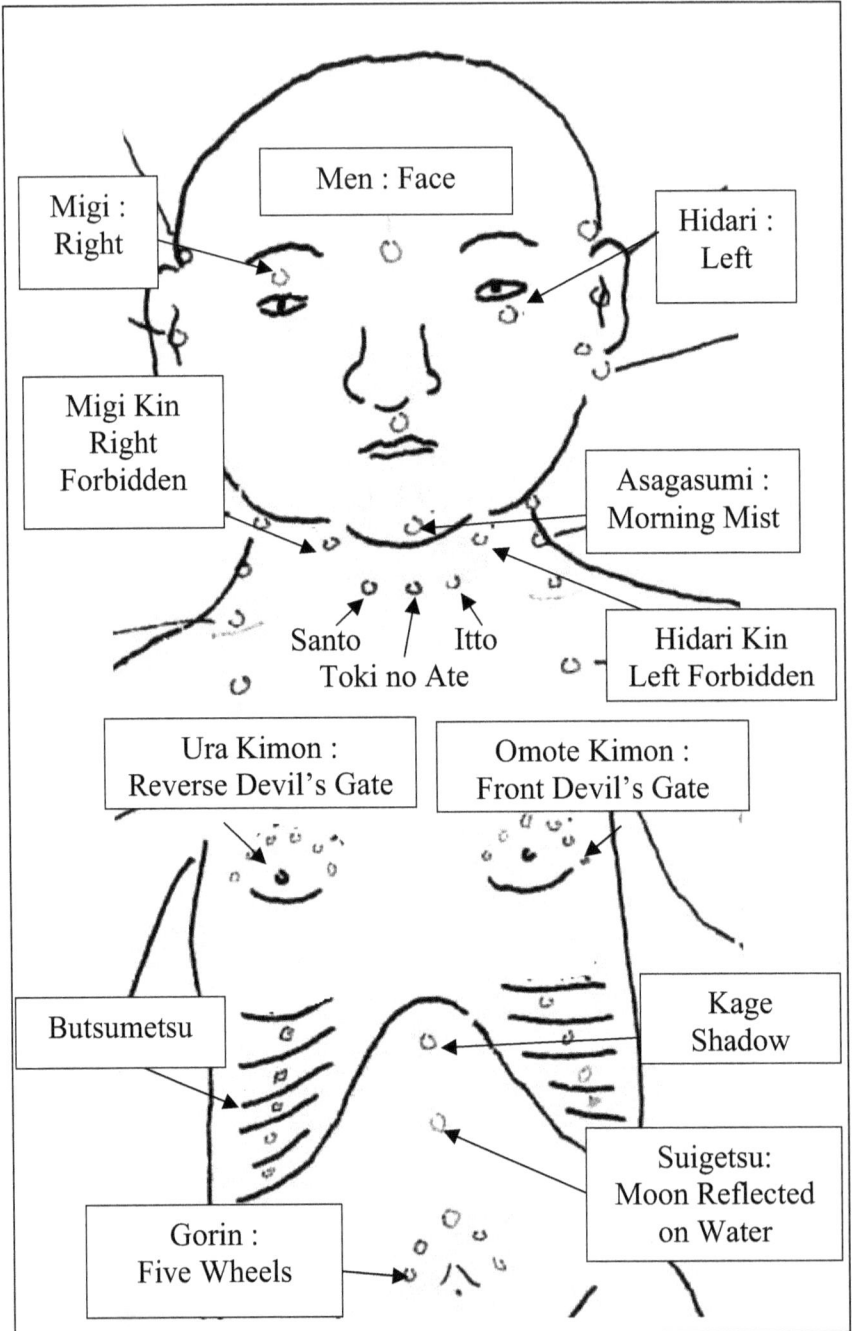

Men : Face

Migi :
Right

Hidari :
Left

Migi Kin
Right
Forbidden

Asagasumi :
Morning Mist

Santo   Itto
Toki no Ate

Hidari Kin
Left Forbidden

Ura Kimon :
Reverse Devil's Gate

Omote Kimon :
Front Devil's Gate

Butsumetsu

Kage
Shadow

Suigetsu:
Moon Reflected
on Water

Gorin :
Five Wheels

Overview

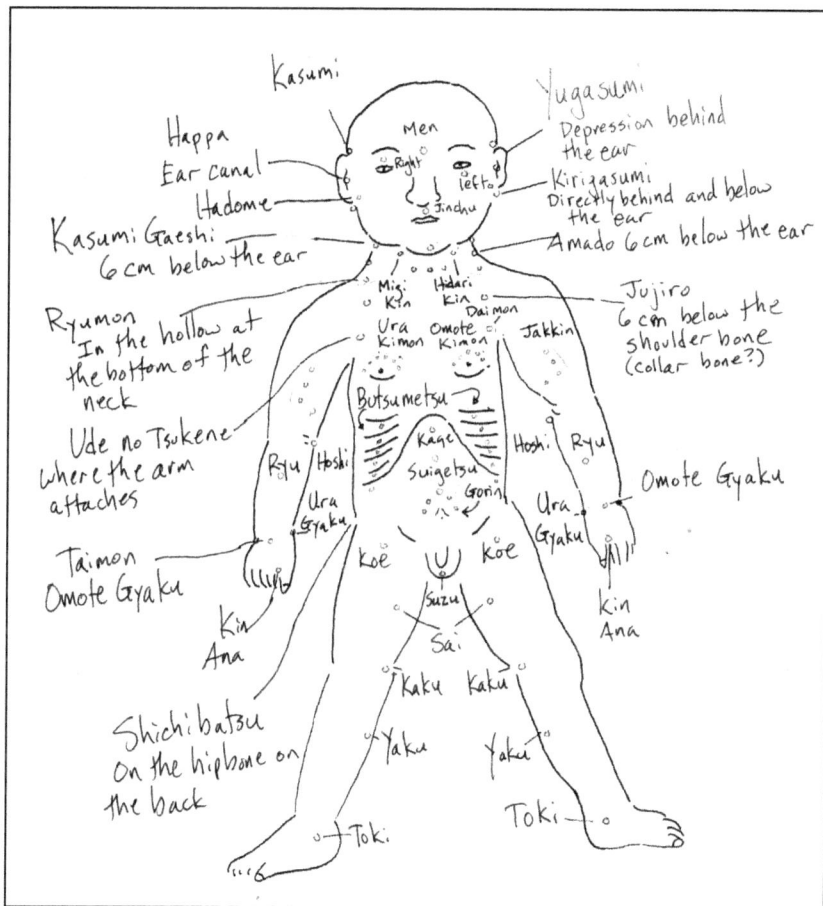

Kasumi

Yugasumi
Depression behind
the ear

Happa
Ear canal
Hadome

Kirigasumi
Directly behind and below
the ear

Kasumi Gaeshi
6 cm below the ear

Amado 6cm below the ear

Men

Right   Left

Jinchu

Ryumon
In the hollow at
the bottom of the
neck

Migi
Kin

Hidari
Kin

Daimon

Jujiro
6 cm below the
shoulder bone
(collar bone?)

Ura
Kimon

Omote
Kimon

Jakkin

Ude no Tsukene
where the arm
attaches

Butsumetsu

Kage

Hoshi   Ryu

Taimon
Omote Gyaku

Ryu   Hoshi

Suigetsu

Gorin

Omote Gyaku

Ura
Gyaku

Ura
Gyaku

Kin
Ana

Koe

Suzu

Koe

Kin
Ana

Sai

Shichibatsu
On the hipbone on
the back

Kaku   Kaku

Yaku   Yaku

Toki

Toki

右虎倒流骨法術無残伝授候也

昭和三拾四年拾二月二十日

虎倒流骨法術

元祖　戸田一心斎　信綱

三代　百地三太夫

二代　百地三太夫

初　百地丹波泰光

百地太郎佐ヱ門

竜口珂主　戸田盛柹　信綱

右虎倒流骨法術無残伝授候也
昭和三拾四年拾二月吉日

This certificate of transmission includes all the techniques in Koto
Ryu Koppo Jutsu without any omissions.
Granted on an Auspicious Day in February Showa 34

虎倒流骨法術 Koto Ryu Koppo Jutsu

とだいっしんさい
元祖 Founders　　　　戸田 一 心 斉 Toda Isshinsai

ももちさんだゆう
百地 三 太 夫 Momochi Sandayu

ももちさんだゆう
二代　2nd Generation 百地 三 太 夫 Momochi Sandayu

ももちたんばやすみつ
竜口城主　百地丹波 泰 光
Takiguchi Shironushi　Momochi Tanbayasumitsu

ももちたろうざゑもん
百地太郎佐ヱ門 Momochi Taro Zaemon

とだせいりゅうのぶつな
戸田 盛 栁 信 綱 Toda Seiryu Nobutsuna[3]

---

[3] 栁…柳の異体字 Note: The Kanji 栁 is a variant of 柳

高松寿嗣翃翁　戸田真龍軒正光　戸田大三郎近敏系　戸田大五郎近秀　戸田新五郎正良　戸田英三郎信正　戸田觀五郎信安　戸田不動信近

とだふどうのぶちか
戸田不動信近　Toda Fudo Nobuchika

とだかんごろうのぶやす
戸田觀五郎信安　Toda Kangoro Nobuyasu

とだえいざぶろうのぶまさ
戸田英三郎信正　Toda Eizaburo Nobumasa

とだしんごろうのぶよし
戸田新五郎信良　Toda Shingoro Nobuyoshi

とだだいごろうちかひで
戸田大五郎近秀　Toda Daigoro Chikahide

とだだいざぶろうちかしげ
戸田大三郎近繁　Toda Daiszaburo Chikashige

とだしんりゅうけんまさみつ
戸田真龍軒正光　Toda Shinryu Kenmasamitsu

たかまつとしつぐうおう
高松寿嗣翃翁　Takamatsu Toshitsugu Uou

神道天心流拳法ヲ三十九代
虎倒流骨法術ヲ十五代祖
宗家 上野澄水

伴

上野澄水

上野

伴

義国信貴

うえの　たかし
伴　上野　貴　　　Tomono Ueno Takashi

ともの　くにのぶ
伴　国信　　　　　Tomono Kuninobu

うえのよしあき
上野義明　　　　　Ueno Yoshiaki

神道天心流拳法第三十九代
39th head of Shindo Tenshin Ryu Kenpo
虎倒流骨法術第十五代祖
15th head of Koto Ryu Koppo Jutsu

うえのちょうすい
宗家　上野澄水　　Soke Ueno Chosui
印影(Offical Seal)